CAPTIVATED LOVE

CAPTIVATED LOVE

A Return to Emulating a Biblical Marriage

FRANTZ & DJENNY LAMOUR

Deep River
B O O K S

Published by
Deep River Books
Sisters, Oregon
www.deepriverbooks.com

ISBN: 9781940269450
Library of Congress: 2015938886
Printed in the USA

Cover and interior design by Robin Black, InspirioDesign

CONTENTS

CONTENTS

PREFACE

It is the heartfelt desire of every human being to have a loving relationship. The need to love and to receive love is inked in our inner beings because we are made in the image of God who is love. For most of us, this deep desire for love propels us to seek after a partner from the opposite sex so that we may experience love to its fullness in a marriage relationship. But divorce statistics and unhappy marriages point to a problem: happiness and love are not guaranteed even after you say "I do"! So how can we be sure to experience love in our marriage?

We wrote this book because we believe your desire to experience love is essentially tied up with your willingness to learn how to become a good husband or wife and your commitment to playing that role in your marriage. Thankfully, God has given us a powerful resource in the Bible, which teaches us what it means to be a good husband or wife according to his design. This book will use the Bible to both provide you with a basic understanding of what it means to be a husband or a wife and to show you how you can apply the knowledge you gain to enrich your life and marriage. This is a practical, biblical guide to the steps you can take in building and experiencing the good marriage relationship you desire.

This book also comes from the wealth of information, experience, and wisdom we have gained in thirteen years of living together in a loving marital relationship, with God as the foundation. The secret of our successful and loving marriage is our intimate relationship with God by faith in his Son Jesus Christ through the indwelling power of the Holy Spirit.

We have organized this book in two parts. Part I addresses challenges men face today that challenge them in their marriages, what it means to be good husbands in a biblical sense, important information men must learn in order to become good husbands, and practical steps they can take to actually become good husbands to their wives.

Part II explores the role of wives. We discuss how a woman can become a good, biblical wife to her husband, with practical steps she can take, and we examine the different aspects of what it means to be a wife in a biblical and practical sense.

We hope that by the time you complete this book, you will have a biblical understanding of what a husband-and-wife relationship is all about, and you will be equipped to apply that knowledge in order to enhance the intimacy in your marriage. God has not left us without a clear picture of what it means to be a good marriage partner. Learning how to live out that picture is crucial to having a good marriage where you can honor and love God by the way you relate to your spouse—and where you can experience the love you desire.

—Frantz and Djenny Lamour

PART I
THE HUSBAND

God made men with the potential of becoming husbands. Regardless of race, age or education, wealth or poverty, almost every man wants to have a great and loving relationship, mainly in the form of marriage. The question is, though, how does a man become a good husband?

We strongly believe that the main reason so many married couples struggle to live joyfully with one another is because of a lack of knowledge. You don't automatically become a good husband just by handing a ring over to your woman and kissing her at the altar. It takes more than that. To help you out, we have written this book to share with you biblical teachings to keep and cultivate the love and friendship you want in your marriage.

This book has been written to help you find the deep connection you long to have with your spouse. In it, we have summarized everything we have learned about marriage from reading the Bible forty-two times from cover to cover and living thirteen years of a satisfying and loving marital experience.

Marriage is a triangular relationship between God, you, and your wife. Everyone involved has a role to play. God's role is to bless your marriage with his presence so that you may have a prosperous, long, and fruitful relationship. Yours is to let him work in you to make you a good husband to your wife in a blessed and lifelong relationship. If you fail to learn how to become a good husband, you will not be able to enjoy your marriage.

It is our heartfelt desire that you and your wife will enjoy the good marriage God created for both of you. Even if you are not yet married, you can learn from the school of marriage—through the Scriptures, through premarital counseling, and we hope through this book—to know what your marriage career will entail. Just as God created females to become good wives for life, God created males to have a lifetime career called "husband and father."

The first part of the book is written from Frantz's perspective. Are you ready to get started? Enjoy reading how to become a good husband!

BECOMING A HUSBAND

*"For a husband is the head of his wife as Christ is the
head of the church. He is the Savior of his body, the church."*
—EPHESIANS 5:23

Marriage is the oldest institution in the world. As long as human society has existed, so has marriage. Through marriage, we look for love. Through marriage, we team up to get through life in the best possible way. But today, it's clear that something has gone wrong. More and more marriages end in divorce. Beyond that, more and more people choose not to pursue marriage in the first place, instead hooking up with multiple dating or common-law partners. Yet, most of us still want a good marriage. Our hearts desire the love and intimacy that can only come from a lifelong, committed marriage relationship.

Given the decline of marriage in the world, it is important for us to know what it means to become a husband. Just saying vows and exchanging rings isn't enough! A complete and biblical view of what a husband is can be stated as *"one who is making a lifetime commitment to live with his wife just as Jesus lives with his church in order to build a marriage relationship whose priority is to glorify God."*

When we become husbands, our primary service to God is to serve our wives. When we become good husbands, our children will have good fathers who become positive role models to them so they can learn from us how to build their own families. But we cannot become godly fathers unless we learn how to become husbands who agree to live with our wives according to God. We must be taught how to become husbands, and God

11

wants to teach us if we are willing to learn. Since God is the Maker of everyone and everything, he instructs us in his Word on how we can and should become the type of husbands he wants us to be to our wives.

My own father chose to bring me into this world by raping my mother. She was humiliated, devastated, and hopeless, and she struggled to raise me as a single mom. However, God is able to work out all things—bad and good—to accomplish his glory. I never knew my human father while I was growing up. He rejected and abandoned me. But my heavenly Father welcomed me into his family through the blood of Jesus Christ. I am glad to call God my Father because he elected me to become his son before I knew him, despite my shortcomings. God turned me into a good husband for my wife and the mother of my own children.

In many families without a father, society becomes the example for children in how to live their lives. I was not the exception to the rule. Since my father was not present in the home and my mother was always working to provide for my basic needs, spirituality and morality were not prioritized in my life. Consequently, I was left on my own to figure out how to live. I elected to live a sinful life, which was the standard of living in my neighborhood. Marriage never crossed my mind, nor the thought of becoming a good husband one day. I thought sexual immorality was the only way of living, and my environment was my only example to learn from. Relationships between husbands and wives were never mentioned in the house. No one ever taught me what it means to be a husband.

Many men share stories like mine. Others are very different, but they still face major challenges that are a part of our culture today. With the various pressures we as men face today, it can be very difficult for us to become godly husbands to our wives. Economic pressures, social pressures, time pressures, expectation pressures, work pressures, and ministry pressures all gang up and make it hard for most of us. But just as God was able to fashion this child of rape into a good husband and father, if we let God be God in our lives, he will help us to overcome even the most difficult pressures and challenges!

The goal of being a godly husband to my wife is nonnegotiable no matter the nature of the worldly pressures I face. The Spirit of God lives in me so that I may become all that God wants me to be to my wife and my children. I dare not give any excuses not to represent God in my family. First John 4:4 tells us, "But you belong to God, my dear children. You have already won a victory over those people, because the Spirit who lives in you is greater than the spirit who lives in the world."

The challenge for us as men is to identify key values that will give us strength to counter a culture and a world that is unbiblical in its very foundation and structures.[1] Among the nonnegotiable set of values are our loyalty to God's Word, our dependence on God, and our commitment to our wives that we will build godly families.

With God, we can exemplify a godly marriage to the world. When we purpose in our hearts to be godly husbands no matter what, we will let God's Spirit empower us to overcome the challenges we face in order not to compromise our relationships with our wives. I am committed to being the husband God wants me to be to my wife, even to the point of death. When my journey on earth is over, I want to hear these words from my Lord concerning my role in marriage: "Well done, my good and faithful servant. You have been faithful in handling this small amount, so now I will give you many more responsibilities. Let's celebrate together!" (Matthew 25:23).

THE HEAD OF THE WIFE

"For a husband is the head of his wife as Christ is the
head of the church. He is the Savior of His body, the church."
—EPHESIANS 5:23

So what makes a husband? In God's eyes, what *is* a husband? Is it just saying "I do" and committing to live in the same house until death do you part? As you might have guessed, there's a lot more to it than that.

We become husbands when we accept the God-given command to be the head of our wives. As our opening passage from Ephesians states, the husband is the head of his wife. What does that mean?

This is the key to a healthy marriage from the man's point of view, so it's important that we deeply understand it. Let me try to illustrate what I believe the apostle Paul meant when he wrote those words:

We all know that a body can't live without its head. Since the loss of the head destroys life, the absence of a husband in his role of head will destroy the life of his wife mentally, spiritually, and emotionally. The human head directs all things for the body. It looks out for the whole body and makes sure it is kept safe and healthy. Therefore, as the head of his wife, the husband does not live for himself but for his wife. A man can live for himself, but a husband cannot. He does good things to his wife to glorify God who gave her to him. The human head carries the brain, nose, ears, mouth, and eyes. As the head, the husband uses his brain to think of godly ways to beautify his wife spiritually and physically; he uses his eyes to see good things to give to his wife and his ears to hear instructions from God to bless his wife; he uses his nose to smell his wife's beautiful body, the bone of his bones and flesh of his flesh. He uses his mouth to praise his wife in private and public and to communicate well with her. The husband does all these things for his wife because he is her head.

I was born in Port au Prince, Haiti. When my mother was fifteen years old, a so-called friend invited her to come to her house. Little did she know that this friendly invitation was going to be the darkest and saddest day of her life. When she arrived at the friend's house, the man who would become my father raped her. When she found out she was pregnant by a man she didn't even know, she was confused and upset about what to do and how to inform her parents. Many thoughts traveled back and forth in her mind, one of which was abortion. As she was about to proceed with her plan to abort this unwanted child, she felt within her conscience that it was not the right decision to make. She said to herself, "You never know what this child might become; let me keep the baby."

When she made that crucial decision, the man who raped her disappeared from her life completely. She carried me for nine months through shameful humiliation. When I was born, she named me Frantz Lamour. *Lamour* is derived from the French word that means love.

My mother assumed the roles of both mother and father by working hard day and night to meet my needs and make sure I could get a good education. Because of her, I was able to finish high school, go to college to get my bachelor's in ministerial studies, and become a graduate student in a counseling program at Palm Beach Atlantic University. My mother believed in me and sacrificed her own needs to give me the opportunity to succeed in life, and I am so grateful to her! But her story illustrates how wrong it is for any man to leave a woman without a head—to force her to make life work on her own. My mother has gone through immense hardship for most of her life because of my father's actions, instead of being loved, honored, protected, and provided for. God designed marriage to work in exactly the opposite way.

Just as the human head leads the body, the husband is to lead his wife and do things for her so that she can be the spouse God designed her to be in the marriage. The husband leads his wife to green pastures, just as Jesus the Good Shepherd leads him. The husband follows the headship relationship between Jesus and his church to establish his own headship relationship with his wife. Ephesians 5:23 tells us this clearly: "For a husband is the head of his wife as Christ is the head of the church. He is the Savior of His body, the church."

God designed us from eternity to become godly husbands for him on earth. He called us in Christ Jesus to live God-centered lives with our spouses. A right understanding of how we become good husbands will bring divine meaning to our marriage relationships. Many marriages have fallen apart because the men were never taught what it means to be a husband. We have been taught how to become teachers, mechanics, doctors, computer scientists—everything except how to become good husbands. Whatever our career might be, it should help us be the husbands God intended us to be in this world. God made us males with the potential of becoming husbands and fathers, yet if we do not learn from God's Word what that means, it is possible for us never to truly become husbands after we get married.

A Man and a Husband

A man and a husband are not the same. As men, we live for ourselves, but once we become husbands, we live for our wives. A man thinks of himself, whereas a Christian husband thinks of his wife and how to please *his* head, Jesus Christ. We please our wives because we are husbands. Paul wrote, "An unmarried man can spend his time doing the Lord's work and thinking how to please him. But a married man has to think about his earthly responsibilities and how to please his wife. His interests are divided" (1 Corinthians 7:32–34).

As "heads," we play a mediatory role between God and our wives, yet we cannot get to God without allowing Jesus to be our head. We look to

Jesus for instructions on how to live and treat our wives. Jesus holds his hands, and the husband holds the hands of his wife. Jesus is the head of all men. A husband is the head of his own wife (1 Corinthians 11:1-3). What Jesus represents to a man is what the husband represents to his wife. A man owes his very existence to Jesus.

Paul writes in Colossians 1:15-18, "Christ is the visible image of the invisible God. He existed before anything was created and is supreme over all creation, for through him God created everything in the heavenly realms and on earth. He made the things we can see and the things we can't see—such as thrones, kingdoms, rulers, and authorities in the unseen world. Everything was created through him and for him. He existed before anything else, and he holds all creation together. Christ is also the head of the church, which is his body. He is the beginning, supreme over all who rise from the dead. So he is first in everything."

The Godhead consists of three distinct persons who are yet one in nature: Father, Son, and Holy Spirit. The Son was the Word, who was with God and was God. And the Word became flesh in Jesus (see John 1:1, 14). Since God made all things through the Son, Jesus is entitled to be the head of all things.

The Head and the Body

God built the woman out of the rib of the man (Genesis 2:22). In other words, our wives are our own bodies. A body is dead without the head, and likewise, the head has no value without the body. That is one of the reasons God said it was not good for man to be alone (Genesis 2:18). Both the head and the body need each other to accomplish the purposes for which they were created.

Headship is not dictatorship. The biblical concept of leadership is not about having superiority over others, but about assuming the responsibilities that God establishes for each of us to accomplish his purposes. In marriage, God does not look at husbands as the number-one person and our wives as the number two. No. He sees two beings (his son and his daughter), both made in his image, living side by side and walking hand in hand in marriage for his glory. Marriage is not a place for the husband and the wife to fight against each other for the leadership role. *Instead, marriage is an entity of unity and mutual dependence in which a husband and a wife work together as one team.* A head and a body are not two entities, but one. Even so, a husband and wife are not two entities, but one. There is a constant battle in most marriages between husbands and wives to determine who is number one or number two. The war for supremacy in marriage is Satan's tool to destroy our marriages. God's method is for the husband and the wife to cleave to one another to become one in flesh, spirit, and purpose.

Headship does not mean we are dictators in our marriages, but loving husbands who make decisions with our wives. We do not dictate to our wives what to do, but we diligently work together for the best interest of the family and of God's kingdom. The Bible teaches that a married couple must make decisions together. God gave us our wives to become our helpers, after all (Genesis 2:18). To ignore the help of God through our wives is like saying, "No, thank you God. I am fine alone." But God said, "It is not good for the man to be alone" (Genesis 2:18).

The Leadership Role

So why do we need leadership at all? Why bother designating a "head"? In every organization and every country, someone must assume the role of leadership in order to plan, organize, direct, and supervise the affairs of the institution so that its goals can be fully realized. A family is no exception. God has set goals for the family. He has established husbands to be the leader so that his plans can be fulfilled.

A true leader is someone who is leading a person or a group of people to an ideal place they cannot go by themselves—for example, to develop better character or to fulfill a goal. Jesus is the perfect example of what the leadership role of the husband should be in relation to his wife. Jesus is the way, the truth, and the life (John 14:16). As a leader who subjects himself to Jesus Christ, a husband should lead his wife to Jesus so she can be like Jesus, she can be with Jesus, and she can live for Jesus. That is the vision a husband has for his wife. He leads his wife according to objective truth, that is, God's righteous standards. Jesus is the personification of objective truth. God's Son became human in order to reveal the truth and to make that truth available to us for application in our lives. Thus, we can become righteous people by practicing the truth. Jesus's words are life and spirit. "The Spirit alone gives eternal life. Human effort accomplishes nothing. And the very words I have spoken to you are spirit and life" (John 6:63). Therefore, to obey Jesus is to have life.

God wants to transform a wife into the likeness of his Son, Jesus Christ: "For God knew his people in advance, and he chose them to become like his Son, so that his Son would be the firstborn among many brothers and sisters" (Romans 8:29). God uses the husband as the spiritual leader through whom he can achieve that goal. Jesus leads the redeemed ones, his church. Likewise, God has entrusted a wife to her husband to exemplify Christ's relationship with his people. Family and society pay a steep price when a husband does not assume the role of leadership in his marriage.

As men and husbands, we must follow our Leader—Jesus Christ. He only can enable us to be the leaders God wants us to be to our wives. We are the visuals through whom our wives can see God's plan for the marriage. As the leaders, we think and plan good things for our marriages in consultation with our spouses. Our method is obedience to the Word of God; our motive is love; our strength and ability is the Holy Spirit. We must step up to the plate to be the leaders that God wants us to be in our marriages. We agree with God to be committed and attached only to our wives.

The spiritual tone of our marriages begins with our leadership as husbands. Everything begins with the leader. We need to make our wives rejoice because we are their head, just as Jesus our head gives us joy.

Headship also means to protect our wives. God calls us to protect the name and reputation of our wives. Our wives do not have to hire bodyguards to protect themselves because God gave them to us to be their protectors. I stand for my wife because I am her husband. My wife does not need to wonder about who is her protector. I am her protector because I am her husband. I, Frantz Lamour, am called by God to protect my wife, and I do it wholeheartedly with his help.

As the head, we ought to protect our wives in everything. We need to protect our wives from the cares of life, from Satan and his demons, from evildoers, from loneliness, from depression, from emotional breakdown, and from anything or anyone who wants to harm them. If we let our wives go without our protection, they will be vulnerable to falling into temptation. The first husband, Adam, did not protect his wife from Satan. Consequently, they lost fellowship not only with God but also with each other, and they were thrown out of their home in Paradise. God came to their rescue and saved them from Satan. Likewise, even if we have failed in the past, God is still able and willing to rescue us from the enemy in order to protect our wives and families. If we have not been the kind of protectors we must be for our wives, we need to let God rescue us from the hands of Satan.

The devil wants to destroy our marriages at all costs. He wants to destroy and kill the love God has poured in our hearts for our wives through his Spirit (Romans 5:5). We dare not give access to Satan to destroy that love with the things of this world. He wants to make us think that our wives are the enemy. No, that is not true! God gave us wives to be our companions and helpers and to make us whole. If our wives are not what they ought to be, then we must communicate that disappointment to our boss, Jesus Christ. We were incomplete without her: "It is not good for the man to be alone. I will make a helper who is just right for him" (Genesis 2:18). God gave us our wives to be our teammates and our friends. Jesus, our coach, wants us to complement each other as players who are on the same team. We cannot afford to allow Satan to score on us. We need to protect the wives God has given to us, or Satan will take them away from us to give to other men. Let us be on our guard!

If we are husbands only in title but not in function, we need to confess our shortcomings to Jesus, our Leader. We need to tell Jesus why we have failed him in not being the kind of head he wants us to be to our wives. Jesus will forgive us and help us be the husbands we should be. If we are husbands both in title and in action, we are blessed to be representatives of God in our marriages. We should be thankful to God for allowing us to respond to the call of Jesus to be good husbands with the help of his Spirit.

When we behave as Jesus expects in our marriages, we will turn our era into a good generation. That generation will produce men and women that serve God. We are channels God wants to use in order to build strong and stable families. Our commitment to becoming good husbands to our wives will also equip us to become good fathers to our children. We will save our families for generations to come. Our children will see in us good role models worthy of imitation. It matters greatly that we assume our responsibility to become godly husbands to our wives, that is, our own bodies.

Attaching to Our Wives

As the head, we represent *life* to our wives. The head must remain attached to the body for the continuity of life. Likewise, it is vitally important that we stay attached to our wives to keep our relationship with them alive. *We should not attack our wives, but attach to them.* Since the loss of the head destroys life, our absence will bring death to our wives. This death can manifest itself in the form of loneliness, depression, discouragement, complaining, sickness, and more.

God knows that our wives need us to live—in every sense of the word. We need to live *for* them and *with* them, really being present with them. God made the wife for the husband. "Therefore shall a man leave his father and his mother, and shall cleave unto his wife: and they shall be one flesh" (Genesis 2:24 KJV). In order for the husband to enjoy his wife, he must *cleave* to her. "Cleave" means to unite, to "stick closely to." It means we need to attach!

God does not expect us to choose between life and wife, but to enjoy life with our wives! "Live happily with the woman you love through all the meaningless days of life that God has given you under the sun. The wife God gives you is your reward for all your earthly toil" (Ecclesiastes 9:9). Some husbands choose between what they do and like and their wives. Consequently, their wives no longer have priority. We must cleave to our wives so we can enjoy life together in whatever activities we do. It is not good to allow anything or anyone to detach us from our spouses. Doing so will ruin our marital relationships. To neglect one's wife is to put her on life support in anticipation of death.

The love in the heart of a husband whose head is Jesus is so great that he cannot help but think about his wife. She is with him in his mind while he is working. He calls her during break time. He just can't stop thinking about the woman he chose to be his wife. A woman feels secure and gratified when she knows her husband is mindful of her. A husband ought to be attached to his wife physically (spending quality time together and becoming one flesh sexually), emotionally (this gives his wife a sense of security), and psychologically (he is always dreaming and thinking about his wife). That is how it was during courtship, and it should not stop after the wedding ceremony. Let the loving attachment continue into marriage!

Go, husbands! We need to let the world know we are obsessed with our wives. Some people may think we are insane, but that is okay. Jesus, your head, loves you. He always thinks about the church, his bride, which you are a part of. He wants us to remain attached to him so we can remain attached to our wives. If Jesus detached himself from the church, the result would be death. Likewise, our wives will suffer much if we separate ourselves from them. We are the head, and they are the body.

Marriage and Ministry

Many wives are dealing with loneliness because we detach ourselves from them in order to be devoted to the cares of life and work or to human ministries. "But ministry is a good thing!" you say. "God wants us to do it!" Yes, but human ministry and God's ministry are different. Human ministry relies on human ingenuity, genius, and strength. Human ministry is man-focused. Human ministry can also keep us away from our family and from God.

On the other hand, God's ministry brings us closer to him and to our family. God's ministry is focused on God and the common good. God's ministry gives purpose, perspective, and meaning to our lives. God's ministry is not for one member in the family, but for the entire family.

The purpose of God's ministry is approaching and knowing God himself. We do all things on the basis of two purposes: to show our love for God and to reveal his glory—that is, his love, holiness, mercy, and might—in our relationship with others.

God's ministry always has the right perspective built into it. By "perspective," we mean the correct order and priority of ministry. God's order is God first, family second, and others last. God's ministry brings satisfaction. Together with our wives and children, we can work for God in his ministry. We do this while attached to our wife, not while separated from her.

Before God and the World

One of the keys to a good marriage relationship is our knowledge about our role and willingness to accomplish our responsibilities as husbands. In the United States, each state has at least one representative in the Senate or in the House to represent the interests of the people residing in their states. Who should represent the family? The answer is obvious—the husband. The husband is the family's representative before God and man.

The Bible gives several examples of husbands who represented their families before God. Consider the example of Job. He always prayed for his children and sanctified them (Job 1:5). As head of his family, he interceded for his children and for any of the sins they might have committed against the holy God. He was very concerned about the spiritual life of his family. Today, many husbands fail to represent their families because they expect the church or some other organization to be their representative before God. The church can help a family, but God never intended for the church to assume the role of the husbands. As the head, we are priests of our marriages before God.

As husbands, we must not only represent our marriage before God through intercessory prayer and Bible study, but we must also represent our marriage before the world. How can we do this? We need at least three fundamental elements: First, a good character, which comes because we allow God's Spirit to control us (Galatians 5:22–23 and 1 Timothy 3:2–3). Second, we must be good leaders of our own homes (1 Timothy 3:4–5). Our leadership within our own family serves as vital criteria for us to be used by God in a greater dimension. We will disqualify ourselves as leaders in society and in our local churches if we cannot lead our families to accomplish God's purposes. We must become loving husbands and caring fathers in our homes so that we can lead other people as well. Third, we must have a good spiritual reputation. Our reputation within the community in which we live is a determinant factor to inform others whether or not we should assume a leadership role in that community (1 Timothy 3:7; Acts 16:2; Romans 1:8, 16:19; Hebrews 11:2).

Our life is meaningful when we know without a doubt that we are in the center of God's will. When this happens, we can say like Jesus in John 17, "We have glorified you by accomplishing the work you have given us." There is no greater satisfaction in life than to do what God has assigned you to do! As a husband, I need to engage myself in doing God's ministry with my wife and my family. If not, I will entangle myself in doing human ministry at the expense of my fellowship with God and my intimacy with my wife. As a husband, my primary ministry is my wife. My ministry to my wife consists of doing for her what my head, Jesus Christ, instructs me to do.

The goal of every Christian husband should be to have a conscience empty of all offenses before God and men. That was Paul's goal (Acts 24:16), and so it should be ours.

We become true husbands when we take up our responsibility to be the head of our own wives. As the head, we are to attach to our wives, protect them, and represent them before God and men. "Therefore shall a man leave his father and his mother, and shall cleave unto his wife: and they shall be one flesh" (Genesis 2:24 KJV). May God help us to be heads he wants us to be to our wives for his own glory!

CHALLENGES HUSBANDS FACE

"Be on the alert, stand firm in the faith,
act like men, be strong."
—1 CORINTHIANS 16:13

I n our formative years, we all faced challenging issues in our lives that seemed to be insurmountable, and yet these obstacles were helpful in making us who we are today. Marriage is not exempt from difficulties. It is crucial to talk about some of the challenges men will have to overcome in order to become good husbands.

Fortunately, God has made provision in Christ Jesus to empower us to win this battle. With God, we can definitely be what he asks us to be because nothing is impossible with him. Because we love our wives, we buckle up and are ready for battle to overcome anything that will come our way and attempt to stop us from becoming good husbands. It is worth saying this to your wife: "Honey, I am ready to not only fight life's challenges for you, but to die for you if necessary with the help of God." First Corinthians 16:13 clearly says, *"Be on the alert, stand firm in the faith, act like men, be strong."*

Challenges to Overcome

The pressures we face from society today are overwhelming. The dominance of the materialistic worldview and the lust after worldly pleasures can make it very difficult for us as men to become good husbands to our wives. The only possible way to win this battle is to rely on God's help to overcome the daily spiritual and material strongholds that are tempting us.

26

In this chapter, we will discuss three main obstacles that can keep a man from fulfilling his role as a husband.

The first challenge is our *career*. We definitely need a career in order to work and provide for the needs of our wives—but this can sometimes make it difficult for us to attach ourselves to our wives as we should. After all, we have to work, don't we?

Oftentimes, our career becomes a tool that Satan uses to keep us away from the women we call our wives. Our jobs can easily become our gods if we forget God who blessed us with the ability and calling to work in the first place! The desire to make money at any cost will keep us away from our lover. *A career does not have to be destructive to our marriages.* Instead, it should be used as a means to build and maintain a marriage relationship. In order to achieve that goal, we must know why we are working.

Some of us have adopted wrong thinking about our careers. We base our significance and security on what we do for a living. Because we are deceived by the devil, we fall into the social scheme of believing that a real man must perform in order to be valuable. Performance-based identity is an easy trap to fall into.[2] We think that we become important because of what we do and possess. Consequently, we become workaholics—to the detriment of our relationships with our wives. We prioritize our careers over spending time with our wives. We consecrate most if not all of our time to getting raises or promotions, while our relationships with our wives go down gradually until we are no longer mentally and emotionally connected with them.

We do this because we have believed a lie from society about who we are and how we get our significance. The biblical truth about significance is this: *God made us in his own image, therefore we are significant.*

As husbands, then, we need to know why we work. The answer is pretty simple: we work for God's glory (Colossians 3:22–24) and for our wives (1 Corinthians 7:32–34). As the head of our wives, we are the main providers to meet their needs. We are working for our sweethearts because we love them!

Once we understand why we get up every day to go to work, our wives will always be with us no matter what we do for a living. No man should work for another man's wife. That will lead to many problems. Every husband is responsible to work for his own wife. When we work for our wives, we actually work for ourselves because our wives are our own bodies. Obviously, we need to take care of our own bodies! Jacob worked fourteen years for the woman he wanted to become his wife. We work for our wives to ensure that their needs are met. Their parents took care of them when they were under their responsibility. Our wives let go of their last name for a new one—*our* last name. Since they agreed, out of love, to bear our names, we should be proud of our wives and work for them. Jesus worked for the church, his bride. Jesus meets every need of the church. He always makes provisions for his followers to accomplish the work of the Father. Since Jesus is our head, we must imitate our Lord. We do not work for ourselves, but rather for our wives.

My daughter Djunia is now twelve years old. When she was nine years old, she told me, "Daddy, I do not have to be concerned about where I will live when I am ready to get married. It is the responsibility of my future husband to buy me a home in which to live. I notice that you as my father take care of me and my sister and my mother because you love us. I pray that God will give me a husband just like you are to my mother." My daughter knows a husband must work for his wife. Bravo, Daughter! May God give you a godly husband!

A husband-father must show his love for his wife and family by working hard to provide for them. God expects that from him. His wife's parents hope to see that as well. The people around him are watching to see if he fulfills that responsibility. If he does not, he will become a disgrace to his family, a blasphemer of God (1 Timothy 5:18, 2 Thessalonians 3:10), and a subject of discussion among the members of his wife's family. Wow! That is a lot to think about. It costs to be the husband, right?

We must provide what our family needs in order for them to function well. Our family should never wonder what they are going to eat or drink, or whether they will have clothing to wear because we are lazy. It is our responsibility as husbands to know how the needs of our wives and our families will be met.

This goes beyond just providing for our family physically. Yes, our responsibility as true husbands is first to provide physical food for our spouses. But according to God's Word, in order to live effectively and thrive spiritually, our wives and children need *both* earthly bread and the heavenly (spiritual) bread that proceeds from God's mouth (Matthew 4:4). Unless we are unfit due to physical sickness, we need to work for our families, and we need to lead them spiritually and teach them God's Word. A healthy family is fed with physical and spiritual bread. A husband-father is the primary means God uses in a family setting to take care of his own.

Our second challenge to overcome is our *camaraderie*. By camaraderie, I mean friends. We need to carefully select our friends so that they do not become blocks that build a wall between our wives and us.

The basis for true friendship is to share common values. The first couple, Adam and Eve, had good camaraderie until Satan came into their marriage. When they chose to take him into their friendship, he destroyed their relationship with each other and with God. We need to keep God at the center of our marriages if we don't want to destroy our friendship with our wives like the first couple did!

Likewise, our selection of friends among the community of God will have an impact on our marriages. If our friends are truly good ones, that impact will be beneficial. Many "giants" will attack our relationships with our wives, and having good friends around our marriage is crucial to overcoming the schemes of Satan.

Friendship requires sharing time and ideas together. If we become friends with people who reject our Christian, theistic worldview, we might not become the husbands God wants. Don't underestimate the power of friends to shape the way we think! For instance, if our friends don't believe in marriage, we might be vulnerable to adopting their worldview. If we don't put on the full armor of God, we can fall for all kinds of things.

The belief systems people hold make and shape their character and conduct. If we keep spending time with people who do not share our beliefs, and/or if we continually listen to their ideas, it won't take long for us to become like them.

Besides God, our wives should be our best friends. It is important that we communicate and spend time with our wives in order to protect and nurture our marital relationship. Jesus, who is our head, does not make friends with the world. He does not embrace their beliefs and values, and as a result, the world hates him. Jesus is light, and the world loves darkness (John 3:19). As we are his followers, the world will hate us and want to destroy our marriages (John 15:18-19).

Being like our Jesus is the only way to live. He chose people who believed in him to be his friends. Friendship with the world is destructive to our marriages (1 Corinthians 15:3, James 4:3-5). We can minister to the people in the world, but they must not truly be our friends until they love the God that we love. We can talk with them, but we must draw a line in the sand so they know what we stand for. We are followers of Jesus. We cannot laugh as they are giving their filthy jokes. We cannot listen and approve of their foul language if we want to build healthy relationships with our spouses. We become what we hear because faith comes from hearing. You are not better than people in the world—just very, very different because you have the mind of Jesus Christ (1 Corinthians 2:16).

Jesus is the best friend the church has. Like the song says, "What a friend we have in Jesus." Our love for our wives should compel them to say, "What a faithful friend I have in my husband! I can count on him." The kind of friend Jesus is to us is the same type of friend we must be to our life companions, our wives.

Our third challenge to overcome is *compromise*. There is much to say here. You do not have to be a historian to see the negative impact on marriage through the ages because of husbands who have compromised their love for their wives. Husbands who compromised their moral integrity have destroyed many families and generations. Husbands who have compromised their loyalty to their wives have caused many pains to children and to society in general. With God's help, we choose not to compromise his presence in us so that we will not put our marriage in harm's way.

Before we choose to compromise who we are in Christ through adultery, dishonesty, or other actions, it is worthwhile to think about the consequences we will pay and the indescribable pains our family will have to bear. The Bible gives us many examples of people who compromised their moral principles and the consequences that followed. For instance, David committed adultery with Bathsheba and murdered her husband. As a result, David and his family suffered much, even though God forgave him (2 Samuel 11, 2 Samuel 12:1–24, Psalm 51). What will our compromise with the world mean to our fellowship with God (see 1 John 1:6–7)?

We are not the head of many women, just one—that is, each man is the head only of his wife. With God's help, we are called to be faithful to our wives. God will judge us if we defile the marriage bed (Hebrews 13:4). God honors marriage, and he wants us to honor our marriage also. When sexual temptations come across our path through any of the perverse means our society accepts as "normal," we should ponder the bad example of David, who took Uriah's wife for himself, and the devastating effects his compromise had on his own family and on God's people (see Psalms 32 and 51, 2 Samuel 12). May the Holy Spirit help us so that we don't compromise God's principles! Any compromise that requires us to violate biblical principles is not a compromise, but corruption.

Let us be wise not to let the lips of an immoral woman bring us to death. Let us pay no attention to the words of her mouth (Proverbs 5). We can be like Joseph, who ran from the wife of his boss, Potiphar, in order to protect his purity (Genesis 39). Running from pornography, impure thoughts, and immoral women is good for our marriages. Remaining true to our wives shows the world that we are committed followers of Jesus Christ. Making love with our own wives is God's plan for us. The Bible says, "Let your fountain be blessed, and rejoice with the wife of your youth.

As a loving deer and a graceful doe, let her breasts satisfy you at all times; and always be enraptured with her love. For why should you, my son, be enraptured by an immoral woman, and be embraced in the arms of a seductress?"(Proverbs 5:18–20 NKJV).

Fighting to keep your marriage pure protects you from becoming sick with sexually transmitted diseases and from contaminating your life with sins, which are not good for your fellowship with God. Commitment is one of the most important moral principles of a happy, strong, safe, and lifelong marriage.

The good news is that you are not alone in overcoming these challenges. God is with you always. You are his son through faith in Christ Jesus. "So be strong and courageous! Do not be afraid and do not panic before them. For the LORD your God will personally go ahead of you. He will neither fail you nor abandon you" (Deuteronomy 31:6).

GIVING LOVE TO OUR WIVES

*"For husbands, this means love your wives, just as Christ
loved the church. He gave up his life for her."*
—EPHESIANS 5:25

*"Love is moral even without legal marriage,
but marriage is immoral without love."*
—ELLEN KEY

*"Love is the thing that enables a woman to sing
while she mops up the floor after her husband has walked
across it in his barn boots."*
—HOOSIER FARMER

*"There is no more lovely, friendly and charming relationship,
communion or company than a good marriage."*
—MARTIN LUTHER

Before God adopted me into his family, I dated many women to align with cultural demands and to satisfy my sexual needs. After I became a child of God, I was afraid of dating because of my past experience of sexual immorality. Instead, I decided to occupy myself in the work of God and to spend my time in prayer, fasting, and studying the Bible. I had no time to look around for a prospective marriage partner. The Spirit of God created within me a desire for God, and my encounters with him provided me more pleasure than sexual pleasure. My mind was so focused on him that his work through the local church became my daily activity. In fact, some people in my church thought that I was a eunuch because I was not interested in dating!

When God saw the time was right to give me a virtuous wife, he matched us together with a simple yet spiritually significant look. One Sunday while I was going to church, I saw a beautiful young woman standing by the main entrance of the church. Though I had worked at the church for many years, I had never noticed her before. That day, God opened my eyes and I *saw* her. At that moment, I thought, "Thank you, God, for giving me my wife!" She later told me that she felt the same way about me at that moment. That is how God brought Djenny and me together to begin our loving journey. God is the perfect matchmaker!

Of course, it wasn't just giving her a ring that turned me into Djenny's husband. My *love* for Djenny turned me into a husband for her, and my love as a husband makes her complete.

I decided to marry Djenny because I love her. She is beautiful to me, and she captivates my affection. I am humbly happy to be the one God has chosen to teach my wife his love. I love my wife with my words, attitude, and actions. I speak words that I receive from the Bible to build her up daily. I tell her, "My love for you is eternal. There is nothing you can do to stop me from loving you." With the Holy Spirit in my heart, my heart is overflowing with an attitude of love toward my wife. I am patient with her. You cannot find patience on the shelf at the store, but patience is the invisible attitude in my heart in my relationship with my wife.

I support and believe in my wife, and I keep no record of her wrongs in my heart against her. She is safe in my heart, and she will be safe there for life. I also open my heart to bless her lavishly with acts of love, such as giving her gifts, massaging her, giving her a bath, cooking for her, spending quality time with her, you name it. I am for any good deed that will translate my love for my wife into action! I thank God for giving me Djenny to love for him. She is God's daughter, and he gave her to me to love until I meet him in glory. My heart is for my wife for life.

I don't say any of this to brag. Far from it! My wife and I got married in 2001, and the first year of our marriage did not start well because of my lack of knowledge of what it means to be a husband. I loved my wife, but I did not know how to translate that love to our marriage as a husband. The absence of my father in my upbringing denied me the privilege of a good firsthand example to imitate. I did not have any male figure in my life who I could call "father" to teach me how to become a loving husband someday. Therefore, I brought into my marriage my own broken understanding about what a husband should be. Finally, in desperation, I turned to Jesus. Because of Jesus, I learned how to be a godly husband to my wife.

The early struggle of my relationship with Djenny did not stop me from pursuing God to help me become the husband he wanted me to be to her. That still has not stopped! My desire for God increases daily with the work of his Spirit in me, and my relationship with my heavenly Father empowers me to become a loving husband to my sweetheart. God teaches me biblical principles so that I will not be to my children what my earthly father was to me, and he makes me become the opposite. I love my children like my heavenly Father loves me. God helps me with his Spirit and his words every day. I owe being a good husband to Jesus, who has taught and trained me. God my Father has likewise become the perfect example for me to learn how to become a father to my children.

God has taught me to be a loving husband. When a wife has a loving husband, people will notice it! She will live happily, and others will see it. A husband who wants a good marriage should learn from God how to love his wife. God's whole method to save the world from sin and eternal damnation is love! He gave his Son Jesus as the ultimate expression of his love for mankind, giving eternal life to whoever puts his or her trust in Christ. The finished work of Jesus Christ demonstrates how much God loves us. Love is essential to save souls. *Similarly, love and only love can begin and sustain a marriage.* The love of the husband for his wife will make him give up all that other men cherish in order to save his marriage and make it strong and beautiful.

The love of a husband for his wife is essential for a happy, healthy marriage. No other motive will be sufficient to drive a marriage to fulfill its purposes. Only the love of the husband for his wife will do it. The husband can earn the trust and respect of his wife only through his love for her. Everything began with love. It was love that inspired the man to ask the woman to become his wife. It was love that brought them together for the wedding ceremony to exchange vows before God and witnesses. It was love that sent the husband and his wife to the honeymoon. It was love that brought them back to their home to start living together. Since the relationship began with love, only love can keep it going. The same love that brought the husband into the life of his wife will keep him together with her.

Human love can sometimes feel insecure, and for this reason there must be an even deeper love underlying our marriages. The only sufficient motivation for a God-centered marriage is the love of God in the heart of the husband for his wife. *Husbands, do not wait for your wife to love or respect you first.* God loved us first, and his love for us won our love for him. Likewise, the husband must love his wife first, and his love for his spouse will win her love for him. No marriage will perish if love is its motive! Love for his wife will lead the husband into a life of hardship and self-denial, just as Jesus entered into for us. And there, both spouses can find real intimacy and happiness together.

A man is a husband when he loves his wife. God gave the church to Jesus Christ, and through him, the church experiences his unconditional love. The church cannot know and live the love of God without Jesus. Likewise, God gave the wife to the husband, and through him the wife will experience God's steadfast love. God expects the husband to be the love-giver to his wife. He made the wife special and precious. Therefore, she needs to be loved by her husband. He commands the husband to love his wife and at the same time equips him with his Spirit in order to accomplish that goal. He made provisions in Christ Jesus so that the husband can love his wife like Jesus loved the church.

Marriage is a stage in which the husband demonstrates God's love. Although the wife also loves, it is the husband who primarily demonstrates God's love. That is the way God designed it. It is costly for a man to become a husband. He must forsake all to love his wife. Jesus forsook the glories of heaven and his divine prerogatives to become a man for the sake of loving us. He wants us to walk in his steps as the husbands of our wives. I am grateful for this privilege! I share with my Lord Jesus Christ the privilege of exemplifying the love of God in my relationship with my wife just as he does in his relationship with the church. There is no greater reward in life than the opportunity to be like Jesus! Jesus loves me, and I love my wife just as plain as that. His love is the reason I love my wife. My love for my wife compels her to love God even more. She looks at me as a gift and at God as the Giver. She does not love me more than God, but she loves God more because he gave me to her as a gift.

The husband needs God's help to love his wife as he should. Love is not the product of self-performance, but rather the fruit of the Holy Spirit. As we cooperate with God's Spirit, he will produce love through us—both for our benefit and for our spouse's. By nature, we do not have what it takes to love our wives as we should. We need to allow the Holy Spirit to control us in order to love our wives without prejudice.

Pure love is of the Spirit. When we are filled with the Spirit, then we will love our spouses. Being filled with God's Spirit is not automatic. If it were, God would not have commanded us to be filled! "Don't be drunk with wine, because that will ruin your life. Instead, be filled with the Holy Spirit" (Ephesians 5:18). God automatically gives you the Holy Spirit when you repent and trust Jesus Christ (Ephesians 1:13–14, Romans 8:9, 1 Corinthians 12:13). However, to be *filled* with the Holy Spirit, you must study, meditate, and obey God's Word. We must also pray with his assistance (Romans 8:26–27).

Love is the greatest mark of maturity for the husband who professes to be a Christian. Jesus said, "By this all will know that you are my disciples, if you have love one for another" (John 13:35 NKJV). Love is the key to bringing unity and harmony into our marriage relationship. Love is essential in the success of all human relationships, but especially in marriage.

A Woman's Greatest Need

What is the greatest need of a woman? We may quickly reply, "Money, sex, education"—and there are good reasons to think of those things. However, there are many women who are very rich, who lead active sexual lives, and who are well-educated, and nevertheless, they are not happy or satisfied. All of these needs are ultimately superficial. A woman's greatest need is deeper.

What does the Bible say concerning a woman's greatest need? The answer is given in Ephesians 5:25: "Husbands, love your wives, just as Christ loved the church and gave himself for her"(NKJV).

Love is the greatest need of a wife. When she feels and experiences love from her husband, all things work together for good in the family. The home becomes a paradise on earth. If a husband wants to show that he is truly a committed Christian, he must prove it by showing his wife that he loves her. God commands that husbands *must* love their wives. The greatest need of the wife is love from her husband. He is called to graciously give the love that he receives from his relationship with Jesus to his beloved wife.

Loving Our Wives in Practical Ways

How should the husband love the wife? He demonstrates his love for his wife in many ways:

First, the husband begins to love his wife when he values her. To give value to our wives means to assign merit or value to them and to verbally express it. Our wives will not know what is in our hearts unless we make it known to them through our character and conduct, and our character is mainly revealed through our words. Jesus said that the mouth speaks from the heart. "A good person produces good things from the treasury of a good heart, and an evil person produces evil things from the treasury of an evil heart. What you say flows from what is in your heart" (Luke 6:45).

One way to express our love to our spouses is to speak sincere words that make them feel loved. Words can either destroy or build life (Proverbs 18:21)—it all depends on how we use them. If our words are used carefully and properly, our wives will live joyfully. In 1 Corinthians 8:1, we read the following words: "We know that we all have knowledge. Knowledge puffs up, but love edifies" (NKJV). Ephesians 4:29 instructs us, "Let no corrupt words proceed from your mouth, but what is good for necessary edification" (NKJV)—that is, say nothing that will not build up your wife.

Loving words build up. To express value to another person is to contribute to the construction of that person's life. The Bible uses the word "edify," which means to "build up." Spiritually, our words edify when they promote spiritual maturity. In the context of a marriage relationship, we edify when we use words that fill up the emotional love tank of our spouses. When we speak to our marriage partners, the words we use should make them feel truly loved by us, and the feeling of this love should impact them on an emotional level. If this does not happen, then we have failed to properly communicate.

Verbal compliments and words of appreciation are powerful communicators of love. Think about the difference it would make in your wife's life if you made sincere statements that communicated love to her. Communicating loving expressions to our wives will make a huge difference in our marriages. Our wives must feel our love, especially in times of conflict. Does your wife feel your love when she disagrees with you?

Money cannot buy a good wife. She is a gift from God. The husband understands that he does not deserve his wife. Therefore, he esteems her. Since he loves his wife, he becomes a servant to her. Love always gives. The husband is primarily concerned about what he can give to his wife so she can be sure of his love. Jesus gives the church every blessing in order to satisfy her needs as proof of his love for her. Likewise, the love of the husband should satisfy the needs of his wife.

Second, the husband should love his wife unto death. If a man does not think that a woman is worth dying for, then he should not marry her. Once a woman becomes the wife of a man, he must be willing to die for her. The husband should never stop loving his wife under any circumstances.

The measure and standard of a husband's love for his wife is clearly revealed in Ephesians 5:25: a husband must *give his life* to his wife. As Christ loved the church and gave himself for her, likewise, the husband must love his wife to the point of giving up everything for her well-being—even his own life. Jesus loved the church and died for her. A soldier loves his country and puts his life on the line for her. So a husband who loves his wife should also be willing to die for her.

Christ's love for the church is sacrificial. At the cross, Jesus paid the highest price in order to acquire his wife, the church. Like Jesus, a husband must be ready to pay whatever price is necessary to win his wife and maintain a loving relationship with her. Jacob worked fourteen years to marry the woman he loved. Husband, are you ready to die to self in order to love your wife? What sacrifice are you willing to make for your wife?

Mutual Submission

No wife would have difficulty submitting her life to her husband if he loved her as much as Christ loves the church! A more balanced presentation is the concept of mutual submission (Ephesians 5:21), that is, the husband submits to the needs and desires of his wife by tenderly loving her (verses 25–32), and the wife submits to the leadership of the husband (verses 22–24). If you engage in the type of sensitive and responsive submission described in these verses, then I think it will be much easier for your wife to engage in her end of the submission. The fact that Paul spends more than twice as much time instructing men about how they are to engage in biblical submission than he does wives (7 verses compared to 3 verses) says to me that we men generally need more exhortation about our half of submission than do wives. Jesus loves his Father. Therefore, he submits to his will, that is, to die for our sins so that we may become righteous people through faith in him. "For He made Him who knew no sin *to be* sin for us, that we might become the righteousness of God in Him" (2 Corinthians 5:21).

I think God makes these two concepts clear for us—husbands' submission to their wives and wives' submission to their husbands is closely related. This same type of mutual submission is reflected in 1 Peter 3:1–7, even though the word *submission* is not used. The Holy Spirit even adds the warning to husbands that failure to keep our end of the marital covenant may result in our prayers being hindered (v. 7). When I understand and submit to my wife's needs and desires, this means I love her. The duty of good husbands is to love their wives. Christ's love for the church is the perfect example. His love is sincere, pure, and constant.

Like Christ, the husband must give himself for his wife. Practically, this means he must be willing to sacrifice his friends, time, pleasures, ambitions, parents, and his own life in order to show his love for his wife. No material thing can compensate for a husband's love for his wife.

Third, the husband must love his wife as his own body. The church is Christ's body. Just as Christ gave himself for his body—the church—so must a husband love the person who becomes his wife in order to keep the sacred bond of marriage. "This is now bone of my bones and flesh of my flesh" (Genesis 2:23 NKJV). When a man and woman get married, they become one flesh (Genesis 2:24). The man who loves his wife loves himself as well.

For a man to love his wife as his own body means that whatever good he does for his own body he should do for his wife also. Remember, he is the head, and the wife is his body. Both the head and the body need each other. To love his wife as his own body means that if the husband always needs money in his wallet, he must allow his wife to have some in her purse also. If the husband does not like to experience any physical threat, he should not threaten his wife. If the husband wants to dress nicely, it is even more important to give the same privilege to his wife, because she represents his body! In other words, everything good the husband wants for himself he must also do for his wife. Here is what Jesus asks of us: "And just as you want men to do to you, you also do to them likewise" (Luke 6:31 NKJV). This principle is fully applicable in the marriage relationship. What a husband wants his wife to do for him, he should do for her. Ephesians 5:28–29 tells us, "So husbands ought to love their own wives as their own bodies; he who loves his wife loves himself. For no one ever hated his own flesh, but nourishes and cherishes it, just as the Lord does the church"(NKJV).

Fourth, the husband should express his love to his wife through nourishing and cherishing her. To illustrate, let me share one of my own experiences with you. One afternoon my wife was not feeling well, and she said to me with a strongly emotional tone of voice, "You do not take care of me." This was her complaining way of asking me for love. I was deeply touched by what she said—so much so that I cried in my heart like a baby. I went outside to clean the car so that I could reflect on her words. I asked myself, "How could she say that I do not take care of her when I faithfully wake up every morning to prepare our two daughters for school, I prepare breakfast for them, I cook for her whenever possible, I work hard to provide for my family so that she does not have to go to work but is able to be with our children . . . I do everything humanly possible to help around the house, but she still feels like I do not take care of her!" It was a very discouraging statement for me to hear. It seemed that everything I had been doing for the family was worthless.

As I prayed to God and thought about her statement, I decided to wait until the storm was over to discover what she meant. When the day was done, like we always do, we prayed with our daughters before putting them to sleep. Once it was just the two of us, I said to Djenny, "You know I love you, and I always help with the children. What you said to me this afternoon was a very painful thing to swallow."

She responded, "I am sorry if I caused you pain. I was just trying to express my feelings to you. I know you help me with the children; you are a good father to our daughters, for which I am thankful. I know you also help cook for the family; that is a good deed on your part. I am grateful that you serve us. But none of those are acts of love. While those are important, they don't demonstrate that you are my husband. When I say that I need you to take care of me, I mean just that: I want you to be my husband."

My wife wanted me to nourish and cherish her. Most wives feel love through the nourishing and cherishing actions of their husbands.

After the conversation, we both laughed about the incident. I have learned that I am not only a father to my children, but more importantly, I am a husband to my wife. I was focused on my responsibilities as a father and a servant, always being willing to help around the house, but I neglected my greatest duty to my wife, which is to be her husband. She would say that for me to take care of her means, "I want you to feed me in bed, to take a bath with me, to touch and embrace me with loving arms, to hold me . . . you name it!" She wants me to leave everything I consider important to focus only on her, especially when she is sick. Since then, I have tried my best to ask my wife how she wants me to take care of her. Now, when I ask my wife, "Can I take care of you?" she just smiles at me and says, "Thank you."[3]

Fifth, a husband loves his wife gently. The apostle Paul understood the importance of being gentle to people as an expression of love for them. He wrote, "But we were gentle among you, just as a nursing mother cherishes her own children" (1 Thessalonians 2:7 NKJV). A husband must be gentle to his wife. The Greek word for *gentle* is *epieikes*, which means *moderation, patient, suitable, fair,* and similar ideas. Therefore, a husband needs to be moderate, patient, suitable, and fair with his wife. Gentleness is the expression of the love of a husband for his wife.

The opposite of gentleness is harshness or bitterness. A husband is not to be difficult with his wife. The heart of the husband must not be filled with bitterness against his wife, because this is ungodly. Living in rigid and punitive ways with your spouse is not gentle but sinful. The gentleness of a husband is the foundation of marital closeness.

The rapport of the husband with his wife should be gentle in words and conduct. In his conversations with his wife, the husband must use just or fair words to express his love for her. Our conduct with our wives must also reveal our love for them. Loving actions can include cooking for your wife, washing the dishes, giving your wife a bath, doing the laundry for her and dressing her up, listening to her thoughts and feelings, being compassionate, and more. The husband must be sensitive in the ways he relates to his wife. It is not rewarding for a husband to raise his voice, yell at his wife, or give her harsh answers. That does not show love for his wife. Instead, that is grieving her. That is making her angry. Love is kind. The kindness of the husband should be the hallmark of his love. God wants the husband to be gentle with his wife. "Husbands, love your wives and never treat them harshly" (Colossians 3:19).

Last but not least, a husband needs to give love to his wife emotionally. So many men think it is wrong to show their emotions to their wives because they were taught that real men should suppress their feelings. This view is not biblical. Men are emotional beings because the God who made men feels and expresses emotion. God shows his emotions in the pages of the Bible: "He is jealous, angry, loving, kind, and grieves over man's rebellion. And we are created in His image. That means, like God, we men feel, and we care."[4] So it is biblical for a husband to show his emotions as an expression of his love to his wife. It does not make him less of a man, but a real man like Jesus. It is perfectly okay for a husband to speak to his wife through his emotions. He can cry for his wife because he loves her. Jesus cried for his friend Lazarus because he loved him and his family. He cried for the city of Jerusalem because he loved the people of that city. He experienced indescribable emotional pains and sorrows for the world when he accepted the will of the Father by dying on the cross for our sins. He was grieved for us because he loved us.

Just like Jesus, a husband can love his wife emotionally. Love from the head is emotionless, but love from the heart has emotions. That means if a husband does not love his wife with his emotions, he loves her from the head only, which can be destructive to their relationship. A husband must love his wife with his head to show his commitment to think of her only, and he must love her with his heart to demonstrate his emotional attachment to her only.

The love of a husband for his wife fulfills God's will for marriage. A man becomes a husband when he loves his wife just as Jesus loves him. Love your wife because God commands you to do so. The refusal of a husband to love his wife is to reject God's commandment to love.

The love of a husband for his wife functions independently of what she says or does to him. He loves his wife solely because God's love abounds in his heart through the Holy Spirit. "And this hope will not lead to disappointment. For we know how dearly God loves us, because he has given us the Holy Spirit to fill our hearts with his love" (Romans 5:5). Today, as men of God who become husbands, we need to make an unwavering commitment to love our wives and then consecrate ourselves to accomplishing that commitment with the help of the Holy Spirit.

I love my wife with no prerequisites. I extend my love to her unconditionally. My love for her is real and practical in my daily living with her. I am committed to my wife. I love her more than anything else in the world. This is the description of the love of a husband for his wife: "I want you to know that I'm committed to you. You'll never knowingly suffer at my hands. I'll never say or do anything, knowingly, to hurt you. I'll always in every circumstance seek to help you and support you. If you're down and I can lift you up, I'll do that. Anything I have that you need, I'll share with you; and if need be I'll give it to you. No matter what I find out about you and no matter what happens in the future, either good or bad, my commitment to you will never change. And there's nothing you can do about it. You don't have to respond. I love you, and that's what it means."[5]

This is divine love, a love that we cannot pay for. This is the type of love that gives a wife pure joy as she lives with her husband. That is the giving type of love that God alone can give to a husband for his wife.

I am so glad and grateful that God saved me with his love through faith in Jesus so that I can love my wife. Loving our wives guarantees the success of our marriages. I like the following quote from Mignon McLaughlin about what it takes to have a successful marriage: "A successful marriage requires falling in love many times, and always with the same person." Whatever a husband says or does, if it does not demonstrate his love for his wife, then he should not say or do it.

Creating Intimacy by Nourishing and Cherishing

When the husband nourishes and cherishes his wife, it will enhance intimacy in their marriage. To love your wife is to nourish her. To *nourish* means to "bring up." Our wives want us to bring them up from their low points. They do not expect us to tear them down or apart. They want our love to always lift them up. It is comforting for the church to know that Jesus always loves her in order to bring her up. Our wives need that same loving support from us. Like Jesus the Good Shepherd feeds the church, we should feed our wives. Like Jesus gathers the church with his loving arm and carries her in his bosom, we should do the same for our wives. Like Jesus leads the church gently to green pastures, we do the same for our wives because we are husbands who follow Jesus.

To love our wives also means to cherish them. To *cherish* is to "keep warm with tender love." The husband is to love his wife with warmth. He needs to foster her with tender care, like a loving mother does her baby. The husband should give his wife reasons to reflect on the experiences they share together as the most important moments of her life. Those moments should always remain with her, even after the husband is gone to be with the Lord. The husband who cherishes his wife like he cherishes his relationship with Jesus Christ will enjoy the blessings of heaven on earth. Nourishing and cherishing our wives creates intimacy.

Here is a question the husband can ask his wife in order to learn how well he is doing in his marriage relationship: "Sweetie, what is the most loving experience you have had because of my presence in your life as your husband?" Some husbands need to pray before they listen to the response of their wives so they do not have a heart attack! We should not take what our wives say the wrong way, but look at their response positively. We need to consider what they say as a means to make things right.

When we fall short of loving our wives as God expects, we need to confess our sins to them for healing (James 5:16) and ask God to forgive us and help us to become loving husbands. With the help of the Holy Spirit, we must make a commitment to cherish our wives from now on. In this way, we can cultivate the kind of intimacy the world dreams about!

Loving Our Wives with True Love

The husband loves his wife simply because she is his wife. He loves his wife as proof of his obedience to Jesus Christ, his head. A husband should not love his wife because he expects something in return from her. That is *phileo* love, which in Greek simply means "a mutual tender affection based upon what we do to/for each other." It is conditional love. This love says, "I will treat you right as long as you treat me right. If you stop treating me right, then I will do the same. My love for you is based upon how you conduct yourself toward me." That is a human type of love.

Nor should a husband's love for his wife only be *eros* love. This love is to want someone sexually. Eros love is when a husband does things for his wife because he wants her sexually. Although sex plays a vital role in a marriage relationship, when a husband loves his wife for the sole purpose of being with her sexually, it is dangerous. The wife will not always be able to make love with her husband. If he only loves her for sexual encounters, he will stop loving her when she can't perform, perhaps due to physical failure or age. Sex is not love but an act of love. When sexual intercourse is no longer possible, love remains because love has no end.

What is left, then? A husband's love for his wife should be *agape* love—true love, God's love. This kind of love says, "I love you regardless of your character or your behavior." It is an unselfish love. This love describes the attitude of God toward mankind. This type of love is the product of a Spirit-filled life. It is not self-performance. Husbands, you will need Jesus in order to have such a pure love for your wife.

Christ's love for the church—his bride—is the divine example for Christian husbands. His objective for the church is twofold: to sanctify her and to make her without blemish. Jesus loves us even though we are not important, good, or obedient. He loves us even though we are definitely not praiseworthy! Romans 5:8 tells us, "God demonstrates His own love towards us, in that, while we were still sinners, Christ died for us" (NKJV). This is what a husband's love for his wife must be as well. He must love his wife despite her imperfections, shortcomings, and weaknesses, just as Christ loves and accepts the husband despite his shortcomings.

Like Jesus, a husband's goal for his wife should be to help her have a spiritual beauty that reflects God's glory. God commands Christian women to have beauty that is hidden in the heart (1 Peter 3:3–4). God prefers to see moral beauty that will never fade away. It is the husband's duty to sanctify his wife by making use of God's Word to teach her in order to present her before Christ without stain.

The action and nature of love is described in 1 Corinthians 13:4–8. We can meditate on those verses to find out if we have this grace; and if we find that we don't have it, we should not rest until we do. This type of love is fully available to us through God, so all we need to do is ask for it and then walk in obedience! This love is tangible proof of a life that is controlled by the Holy Spirit. Love is the fruit of the Spirit (Galatians 5:22), and the Holy Spirit pours God's love into our hearts (Romans 5:5).

When the principles of love are followed, many problems in marriage will disappear. Homes will be happy in Christ. Marriages will be places of rest, peace, and intimate connection. Satan has deceived many people by leading them to believe that they can simply fall in love and get married, and that will make them happy forever—without being mutually committed to nurture the love throughout the course of the relationship in order to stay in love. Falling in love can take place in a moment, but staying in love requires a lifetime commitment to being filled with the Holy Spirit day by day.

Wherever there is mutual love, divorce will not even be an option. Love is eternal. "And now abides faith, hope, and love, these three; but the greatest of these is love" (1 Corinthians 13:13 NKJV). "Husbands love your wives and do not be bitter toward them" (Colossians 3:19 NKJV). Love has no end. Likewise, a marriage relationship with love as its foundation has no end except when death separates the spouses.

Jesus is the perfect model of love (John 15:12–13 and Ephesians 5:1–2). As Christians, if we really want to know how to love our wives, we need to read about the life of Jesus Christ, found especially in the gospels (Matthew, Mark, Luke, and John), to learn how he showed his love for others while he was on earth. We will discover that Jesus healed, served, fed, forgave, touched, showed mercy, and even cried for people. He is the perfect model of love. Keeping our eyes on the Lord Jesus will help us know how to love our wives.

As you read about his life, give undivided attention to the ways that Jesus related to others during his ministry on earth. As we follow Christ Jesus, we will surely love our spouses. Jesus does not ask us to do anything without first giving us the means and the example of how to do it.

Pointing to the Person of Christ

Like everything else in the Christian life, marriage is bigger than we are. It's not just about us being happy, even though it can bring great happiness into our lives! All relationships find their significance and purpose when we become followers of Jesus. When a husband loves his wife, he is saying to the world, "I am a follower of Jesus Christ." Our love for God should be the basis of everything we do in our marriage. "Following Christ is a relationship that drives and defines all we are and do. In fact, that's what I love about followership. It is not a project. It is a Person. It is a relationship to a Person who perfectly loves and cares for us and who is wise beyond comparison—a Person who has done so much for His followers that they look for ways to please and obey Him."[6]

If a marriage is unwanted and a wife is complaining and overwhelmed, most likely her husband does not love her as Jesus commands him to do, or perhaps he does not love her in the ways she feels love. No wife in her right mind will reject marriage if a husband loves her like Jesus loves the church. "So now I am giving you a new commandment: Love each other. Just as I have loved you, you should love each other. Your love for one another will prove to the world that you are my disciples" (John 13:34–35). We ought to love our wives as Jesus loves us so that we may show the world that we are his disciples. We are husbands because we love our wives.

In order to legally make a transaction, we must first deposit money in a bank. If we do not, and we sign a check without provision, we will be disappointed and penalized by the law. This works out in marriage as well. For example, our wives are commanded by God to submit to us as their husbands. Submitting to us will be much easier for our wives if we deposit our love in their hearts first! With that secured deposit of love, though nothing is guaranteed in return from a human perspective, there will be enough provision for them to be submissive.

Jesus loves first, and we love him back through our obedience. What works for our relationship with Jesus will also work for our relationship with our wife. Reasonable commands require reasonable provisions. Jesus made provision first for us when he died and resurrected from the dead. Then he asked us to be his witnesses with the indwelling and controlling power of his Spirit. We can follow his example through our sacrificial love for our wives.

Now, don't misunderstand. We are not saying that anyone's obedience to God is conditioned on what someone else does to us. What we are saying is that if we are faithful to love our wives, it will make the discipline of submission more enjoyable for our wives to practice. Loving help from us will not hurt at all, but will stimulate or influence our wives to submit to us.

Nevertheless, we do not want to play the waiting game to see who is going to obey God first. Sometimes husbands and wives want one to obey first, and then the other will follow through. The husband says, "If you submit to me, I will love you," or the wife says, "If you love me, I will submit." That is simply selfishness on the part of both individuals. It is neither the husband's nor the wife's responsibility to tell the other what to do. That right is reserved to God, who calls the show. Whoever loves God will obey him regardless of what someone else does or does not do. Marriage is made of three individuals: God, you, and your wife. You play your part by loving your wife. Then let God help your wife to do her part.

Making love last in your marriage is God's priority, and it should be for you also because his Spirit is in you to produce love through you. "But the Holy Spirit produces this kind of fruit in our lives: love, joy, peace, patience, kindness, goodness, faithfulness, gentleness, and self-control. There is no law against these things!" (Galatians 5:22–23).

GIVING HONOR TO OUR WIVES

"In the same way, you husbands must give honor to your
wives. Treat your wife with understanding as you live together.
She may be weaker than you are, but she is your equal partner
in God's gift of new life. Treat her as you should so your
prayers will not be hindered."
—1 PETER 3:7

We know that we are truly husbands when we honor our wives. I honor Djenny because she is my wife. I show my honor for her by giving her my best words and behavior. I dress up for her, and I give superlative effort in everything I do for her. She deserves my respect. I honor her because she is special to me, and I deal with her in delicate ways. People around me know Djenny is my wife because she gets my attention as the woman I honor *as* my wife.

God made me a male with the potential to become a husband. But it is giving honor to my wife that makes me her husband in the truest sense. As a husband, I am called to give honor to my wife. Dishonoring my wife means dishonoring God, who gave my wife to me.

Why should the husband honor his wife? The Scripture quoted at the beginning of this chapter tells us that she is a weaker vessel. Every house has weaker vessels in it. Wine goblets are a good example. These are glasses we don't use all of the time. They are special vessels that are secured and used for special occasions and honorable guests. The wife is a "special occasion" for her husband. Stated another way, she is always an "honorable guest." She was a special occasion and an honorable guest before and during courtship. She was the celebrity at the wedding ceremony. She remains a special occasion after the wedding. In fact, she becomes even more special in the marriage relationship! As a wife, she does more good now to her husband than she could do before marriage. Love could not explore its fullness during the courtship. Now, in marriage, there is no restriction to the discoveries and exploration of love for one another that husband and wife can make. God made the wife a special vessel in order that the husband can give her honor.

The husband honors his wife in many ways. *First, he honors his wife by acknowledging her value.* The wife is invaluable to the husband. Think about the first man God created. God made Adam perfect in every way. God made a perfect home for him, called Paradise. God had a perfect relationship with him. Yet God said, "It is not good for the man to be alone" (Genesis 2:18). This speaks of the value of a wife in the life of a husband. Even God's presence and life in Paradise could not replace the presence of a woman in Adam's life! Don't ask me to give a theological explanation. One thing is clear and evident: God said man was lonely in spite of everything he had. When God made man, something was missing. In his love, God satisfied that need by providing him with a wife.

The wife is good to the husband because it is not good for him to be alone. The husband does not deserve his wife. She is a gift from God to him. Proverbs 18:22 says, "The man who finds a wife finds a treasure, and he receives favor from the Lord." The husband expresses his gratitude to God for that gift when he honors his wife. To honor one's wife is to honor God, because he is the one who gives the wife as a gift to the husband. A gift is to be received with gratitude because it is an act of love on the part of the giver. God loves man. Therefore, he gave a wife to man. Man should be thankful to God for his wife.

Second, the husband honors his wife by respecting his wife. The husband absolutely must respect his wife. To respect someone or something is to have a high opinion about it. Respect is shown in many practical ways. First, the husband respects his wife with his spoken words. He speaks kindly to his wife because she is to be respected. He monitors the tone of his voice when speaking to her. Because he respects her, he does not yell at his wife or criticize her. The manner in which he carries on a conversation with his wife will prove if he is showing her respect. The husband's admiration for his wife will not allow him to demonstrate a disrespectful attitude toward her.

A man knows how to respect his superiors at work. He speaks to his supervisor with reverence and respect. Likewise, a husband knows how to respect his wife at home. Of course, there is a major difference: The man shows respect to his boss perhaps because of his position and also because he does not want to lose his job. He wants a paycheck. The husband shows respect to his wife not because she is his supervisor or can reward him somehow, but because he loves her. If a husband loves God and his wife, he will honor them both. We usually honor what we love, don't we?

Honoring our wives makes us their husbands indeed. To honor them, we speak words that communicate good things about our wives both at home and in public. Because we honor our lovers, we present them to others with class and an upbeat heart. We are not ashamed to display our love for them publicly because we are their husbands. We make sure that everyone knows that our wives are a gift from God and that we are thankful to him for blessing us with godly wives. We want everyone to know that the women next to us are our wives by the way we honor them. We hold their hands to make them feel our love through physical touch. We push the shopping cart for them and open the door of the car to show others that we honor our wives and that they are our queens. Just as Jesus came to serve us because he loves us, we also serve our wives because we love and honor them.

Isn't it beautiful to be a husband? Yes, it is! The husband has the privilege of honoring his wife in order to draw people to God, who gave her to him. Jesus honored God the Father with his life during his earthly ministry. His life influenced people to honor his Father. His character and conduct were always aiming to honor his Father. Likewise, the husband must always honor his wife because he is following his Lord Jesus Christ. The husband gives honor to his wife because she is special and an heir of the grace of life in Christ with him. "Husbands, likewise, dwell with them with understanding, giving honor to the wife, as to the weaker vessel, and as being heirs together of the grace of life, that your prayers may not be hindered" (1 Peter 3:7 NKJV). The value of a wife is fixed. She is a gift from God to her husband. To dishonor her is to dishonor the God who gave her to the husband. To honor her is to honor God.

Third, the husband shows respect to his wife by displaying a positive attitude toward her. Attitude deals both with the character and the conduct of the husband. The attitude of the husband toward his wife should be Christlike and demonstrated in Christlike conduct. Jesus does not have a bad attitude toward people, even those society might consider the worst sinners. He is compassionate, loving, forgiving, and considerate toward us all. Since Jesus is the head of every man, the husband should look up to Christ in order to know how to relate to his wife. Sinners loved to come to Jesus to hear him speak because he was kind (Luke 15:1-2). The husband should have the mind of Christ Jesus and always welcome his wife in the same way the Lord welcomes him. The conduct of the husband toward his wife should be gracious and loving.

Fourth, the husband honors his wife by spending time with her. We like to spend time with people we honor. To spend time with your wife is to enjoy being with her—beholding both her spiritual and physical beauty, appreciating what she represents to you, rendering to her the affection that she deserves, and cherishing and nourishing her. "Live joyfully with the wife whom you love all the days of your vain life which He has given you under the sun, all your days of vanity; for that is your portion in life, and in the labor which you perform under the sun" (Ecclesiastes 9:9 NKJV).

Fifth, the husband honors his wife by being faithful to her. When we married our wives, they agreed to trust us with their lives for the duration of their lives. To signify that trust, they gave up their fathers' last names to take our last names. As a result, we cleave to them as their loving husbands. We honor our wives when we remain faithful to our marriage vows to have sexual intercourse with them only. We will sin against God if we betray the trust our wives have placed in us as their husbands.

Sixth, we honor our wives by doing things for them. Some of the things we can do include buying gifts, cooking, throwing a party, writing romantic letters, and giving them an opportunity to spend time with their friends. The sky is the limit! When we do loving acts for our wives, they will know that we honor them, and they will want to be with us.

Seventh, the husband honors his wife by praying for her. When we pray for our wives, we honor them. Calling on God on behalf of our wives is an act of honor toward them, because it shows that we love them. Our wives are grateful to know that we care enough to bring their needs to our heavenly Father in prayer.

It is true that mutually honoring one another in marriage is vital for the well-being of the relationship. Nevertheless, the Scripture quoted at the beginning of this chapter places the responsibility to give honor primarily on the *husband,* not on the wife. Honoring one's wife is not an option, but an imperative. God says, "You husbands must give honor to your wives." Our wives deserve our honor because God commands us to give it to them. When there is a lack of honor in marriage, the love of the husband is poisoned by sin.

PLEASING OUR WIVES

"I want you to be free from the concerns of this life.
An unmarried man can spend his time doing
the Lord's work and thinking how to please him.
But a married man has to think about his earthly
responsibilities and how to please his wife."
—1 CORINTHIANS 7:32–33

As husbands, we live to please our wives. I do all I can to make Djenny happy in the Lord because I know my heavenly Father wants her to rejoice always. I constantly ask my wife to tell me how to please her as a husband. I make it my daily goal to give pleasure to my wife, and if I fail in my mission to please her, I ask for forgiveness. The efforts I put into satisfying my wife create a deep intimacy in our marriage because she knows that I live for her and she lives for me.

To please means to give enjoyment and pleasure or to make happy. God adopted us into his family to learn from him how to become husbands who make our wives happy. Paul said it this way: "But he who is married cares about the things of the world—how he may please *his* wife" (1 Corinthians 7:33 NKJV). If a man does not want to be his wife's pleaser, he should choose to be unmarried like Paul, who wanted to be without care in order to please the Lord only. Paul said, "*It is* good for a man not to touch a woman" (1 Corinthians 7:1 NKJV). However, he goes on to say that if a man decides not to get married, he should remain sexually pure. If he can't do so, he must have his own wife (see 1 Corinthians 7:2 and the rest of the passage). In other words, if God does not give us the gift of celibacy, we are eligible to get married. Once we decide to get married, we are in the marriage to please our wives.

On April 11, 1980, my mother emigrated from Haiti to the United States in search of a better life. I was eleven years old. She hoped to be able to provide for her children better in the future, though she could not bring us with her then. Little did she know that her efforts to transition would bring more instability and insecurity into my life. The absence of my mother became the root of many challenges for me, opening the door for destructive behavior and poor choices. Life became more difficult without her presence. I did not know what to expect after my mother's departure, and I was confused and afraid of the unknown. I was forced to become a man in the eyes of the world, making decisions for the course of my own life and those of my younger siblings.

My grandmother and aunt became my primary caretakers, and my mother consistently sent money to them to provide for my basic needs. They raised me according to what they knew about raising a child, yet the need for a male figure kept growing deep inside of me. Their godless lifestyles hindered and decreased the development of my potential to truly become a man someday. God was with me, but I did not know about him. God knew me before I knew him, and he found me when he was not even a thought in my mind.

In 1986, six years after my mother left for the United States, someone invited me to go church. After I heard the message, God brought this rebellious child to his knees and adopted me into his family. For the first time in my life, I had someone I could call "my Father." I did not know my earthly father until I was about twenty-two years old. He died six months later. In Christ Jesus, I now had a new Father I could call my "Daddy." My Father God found and accepted me into his family while I was dead in sins. I didn't care about him, but he loved and cared for my life. Even when I was dead in sins, he showed forth his love for me through Jesus Christ my Savior and Lord. My sense of self-value is all in my God and Father!

I tell you this story because if you feel like you can't please your wife or learn to live your life in a good way, I want you to know there is hope! I did not know that my encounter with Jesus and his words would change the child conceived through rape and raised without a dad into a good husband and father. Yet, that is exactly what has happened. My relationship with God influences me to be a responsible husband and father for the welfare of my wife and family. Jesus has become my only role model in order to become a good husband, and I am learning every day from him, through the leading of the Holy Spirit, how to be all God wants me to be to my wife. I am humbly honored by the undeserved privilege Jesus gives me of exemplifying my relationship with him through my relationship with my sweet wife.

Gratifying Our Wives and Pleasing God

In order for us to make our wives happy, we need to find out what is going on in their heads. We need to listen to their complaints, romance them in nonsexual ways, massage them (especially their feet), write a letter or poem, use loving words when chatting, make them feel special (doing special things for them such as giving flowers or throwing a surprise party), or take a walk with them in the cool breezes. Through talking with your wife, you can ask her what makes her happy—what she likes. These are some of the things we can do to please our wives. But most importantly, we should ask God, who gave us our wives, to show us how to please them. Since God commands us to give joy to our wives, he will definitely help us find the right way to do it.

We did not marry to gratify ourselves, but our wives. A man who is unmarried is concerned only for the things of the Lord because he has no marital duties or obligations. But he who is married gets things from this world and does things in this world in order to make his wife happy.

It's important to point out here that the husband does not please his wife at all costs. *His first allegiance is to God.* If his wife asks him to do something that violates God's higher law, the husband must choose obedience to God. If pleasing his wife goes against God's law and would cause him to do something wrong against her, the interests of the family, or his relationship with Jesus, the husband should remain faithful to the written standards of God in Scripture.

The ramifications of amusing one's wife at the expense of obeying God's Word are devastating. For instance, Adam decided to satisfy his wife by eating the fruit, and he brought death to his family and the entire human race. He died both spiritually and physically. Spiritually, he died to God. He stopped being connected to his Creator. Because of that wrong choice, he was on his way to the second death, that is hell, until God stepped in to redeem him and his wife. Physically, he separated his body from his spirit. Since Adam is the representative of the human race, his choice to please his wife rather than obey God makes "all people sin and fall short of God's glory" (Romans 3:23). But God's love and grace imparts his righteousness to us through faith in Jesus Christ (see Romans 3:21–26, 5:12–21).

Satan can influence a wife or husband to sin against God. In the case of Adam's family, the devil first deceived Eve, and she fell into transgression. Then she encouraged her husband to do the same, and he listened to his wife. (See Genesis 3 for the full story.) We have many examples in the Bible of couples who chose to gratify each other rather than please God. I think about Abram, who listened to his wife, Sarah, when she encouraged him to make love with her servant. She wanted another woman to do for her husband what she could not do for him. She could not give her husband a child. Guess what? Abraham obeyed his wife. The consequences of that choice are still evident today between the descendants of Isaac and Ishmael. But thankfully, God rescued the family of Abraham (see Genesis 16, 21:1–20).

I also think about other husbands in Scripture who would rather please their wives than please God. Among them we have Ahab, the husband of Jezebel. She turned her husband away from the only true God to worship Baal (see 1 Kings 18–22 and 2 Kings 9:22, 30–37). She stirred up her husband to do evil, and tragically, he heeded her voice. We see in the Bible how influential wives can be! The holiest man, Adam, became sinful because he obeyed his wife. The strongest man, Samson, sinned and died a tragic death because he obeyed his lover. And the wisest man, Solomon, worshiped false gods because he listened to his many wives. (See Genesis 3:1–7, Judges 16, and 1 Kings 11.) We encourage all wives to be wise in what they want their husbands to do so they will not influence their husbands to sin against God.

Godly wives will be pleased when they and their husbands serve God together. Wives like Queen Esther love working with their husbands to accomplish God's plan, as she did in order to save God's people from Haman's conspiracy to destroy the Jews. Esther was pleased when her husband granted her request to protect her people from the hatred of Haman. Most wives will be happy if their husbands serve God with them, like Zachariah and Elizabeth, who "were both righteous before God, walking in all the commandments and ordinances of the Lord blameless" (Luke 1:6 NKJV).

Many wives would love to have a husband like Joseph. He planned to divorce Mary because he thought she was carrying a baby for someone other than him. But later, when Joseph was told by an angel that his wife was doing the will of God, he changed his plans and agreed to remain with his wife. In other words, Joseph pleased his wife because she was pleasing God (see Matthew 1:18–25). Many wives are praying and hoping that their husbands will attend church with them, pray with them, get involved in ministry in the body of Christ, and share Jesus with the world alongside them. They would love to see their husbands let God use them as a preserving influence in the world to slow down the decay of sin (see Matthew 5:13). They would be pleased if the quality of life their husband lived made people in the world thirsty for the living water that only Jesus offers. We can please our wives by serving God together with them.

Pleasing our wives is our duty, but we must please them within the boundaries that God set in the Bible. Let us do so with all our energies and efforts!

PRESERVING OUR WIVES

"For the husband is the head of the wife even as Christ is the
head of the church, his body, and is himself its Savior."
—EPHESIANS 5:23

"The LORD keeps you from all harm
and watches over your life."
—PSALM 121:7

As males, we become husbands in the truest sense when we preserve our wives. In fact, God keeps us from all harm in order that we may preserve our wives. As Ephesians 5:23 states, Jesus is both the head *and* the Savior of the church, his body.

The words "savior" and "preserving" work together in the redemptive work of Jesus Christ. As sinners, Jesus saved us from our sins, and as his followers, he keeps us from sinning to preserve the good work that God began in us at conversion (John 10: 28–30, Philippians 1:6, 1 John 3:8–10). He saves and preserves his relationship with his church through his words and Spirit. And since marriage was designed by God to reflect the relationship between his Son Jesus and the church, *he saved us to become husbands in order to preserve our wives.* God has saved and equipped us with his Spirit to be for our wives what Jesus is for his bride, the church.

Who should preserve my wife? I should, as her husband. Preserving my wife is my duty. I am her preserver, and everyone should know that. So what does that mean? What does "preserving" or "saving" a wife look like in our day and age?

The instances in which God uses me as a husband to preserve my wife are countless. I preserve her from beliefs of low self-esteem that have resulted from how she grew up as a child. I encourage her to be all that God wants for her in every level of life, and she rises to that encouragement. I complete her as her husband. The dangers that my wife faces daily fall on my shoulders. I do not allow her sins against God and me to make me judgmental toward her. Instead, her sins give me the privilege of protecting her from the defilement and guilt of sin with my love and forgiveness. My spouse does not have to defend herself against the attacks of others or against life's challenges because God has placed me in her life to uphold her just as Jesus upholds me. Jesus is the Savior of the world. But me, I preserve my wife.

My wife is proud of me because I keep her safe. My job is to rescue my sweetheart with humility and kindness when she falls. This has amazing results in my own character as well. The judgmental and critical attitude I had toward sinners before marriage are gone. The institution of marriage demands that I preserve my wife, and I have been doing my duty of preserving her with the help of the Holy Spirit. This changes me as well as serving her.

Djenny explains my work of preservation this way:

"My husband preserves me as his wife with the words he uses when we are communicating with one another. He speaks loving words that build me up and promote my personhood. He reassures me daily how much he loves me through his words, character, and conduct. He does not use foul language when he is chatting with me, for which I am grateful to God, for I know that if God did not cleanse his heart, I would be the first one to bear the consequences as his wife! Another way my husband saves me is by helping me to rest physically. As women, we are always overworking and never finding time to rest, but my loving husband does things around the house and thus gives me time to take care of myself, to be with my friends, and to step out with my daughters. Furthermore, he is saving me by showing me love and affection to keep me from fulfilling those needs outside of our marriage. I would also say that his love for the Bible has influenced me to read God's Word daily. Those are just a few examples of how my husband preserves me as his wife. I thank God for my husband every day, because only he could give me such a godly man!"

When a woman becomes a wife and a mother, she has a heavy load of responsibilities to carry in the family and beyond. She meets the needs of her husband: food, clothes, attention, sentimental needs, and more. She also meets the needs of the children: food, clothes, physical cares, homework, playing time, school meetings, library visits, and loads of emotional support! On top of all those activities, many women have to take care of the needs of the house: cleaning, shopping, cooking, washing, serving the meals, washing the dishes, and so on. Oftentimes, the wife has to work outside the home also. Furthermore, the wife has to be prepared to welcome special guests and family members.

Looking at many women as they struggle to maintain all of this, I have to ask, where are their husbands in all of these pressing needs of life? The children are the seeds of the husband. The wife carried each child for *nine months,* and often we men complain if we have to take out the garbage for five minutes! We need to help save our wives and our own children. We do that for ourselves and out of love for our wives. If I may use the analogy, sometimes the daily grind of life can make it seem like a woman is on life support and about ready to die. She has no time for herself—not even to talk to her friends. We must support our wives in these situations. We cannot stand on the sidelines just watching what they are doing without giving any help. We cannot be passive in the marriage. We love our wives. They carry our last names. Actively teaming up and working together with our spouses is good for our marriages. This shows that we are men who have become loving husbands.

Jesus is the Savior of the world. We, on the other hand, are called to rescue our wives and be their lifesavers. We cannot afford to try to save the world at the expense of our relationship with our wives. We are not called to be saviors of the world! There is only one Savior, Jesus Christ. Let me say it again: husbands, *don't try to save the world*—that is the job of Jesus Christ. Our primary responsibility to the world is to let God use our love for our wives to influence others to come to Jesus Christ. Our marriage relationships are to be the spheres where God reveals himself to the world. As Christians, we know that God called us to preach about his kingdom to all nations. Yet we are more than Christian men—we are Christian men and husbands. Our primary ministry is to our wives. We should save our wives, and together we can make the world thirsty for Jesus, the living water.

After Paul met Jesus on the road to Damascus, the Lord showed him the road map of his life. He explained to Paul in detail what the rest of his life would be like after his encounter on that road (Acts 9:1-30). Having understood the scope of his life mission as given by our Lord Jesus Christ, Paul thought it would not be fair to have a wife by his side. After Jesus told him he would suffer, Paul concluded it would be too much to put a woman through. He had the right to have a wife (1 Corinthians 9:5), but he chose not to be married because of what he needed to do for the Lord. Paul understood that the primary responsibility of a married man is to his wife: "But I want you to be without care. He who is unmarried cares for the things of the Lord—how he may please the Lord. But he who is married cares about the things of the world—how he may please his wife" (1 Corinthians 7:32-33). The husband pleases his wife in the Lord.

Setting Our Wives Apart

Husbands also become saviors to their wives when we use the Word of God to set our wives apart from ungodly women—that is, to make them different from the women of the world. The Word of God has the cleansing power to make our wives spiritually beautiful just as God wants them to be. Jesus cleanses his bride, the church, with the washing of his Word. Jesus makes his Word available to us to cleanse our wives just as he cleanses his bride, the church (Ephesians 5:25-30). What a challenge we have as husbands! God expects our wives to be spiritually beautiful (1 Peter 3:3-4), and he holds us at least partially responsible for making sure that happens!

So what does this mean practically? It means that we share together the teachings of Jesus. God's Word saves and purifies. God wants us to be the saviors of our wives in the sense that we keep them from sinning against God because we study and understand the teachings of Scripture together. The husband is the pastor of his wife. We need to help our wives be different from the world; in other words, to sanctify them with the Word. To sanctify our wives is to present them as a loving offering to God. That means we help them be different in word, action, conduct, and character by the way we implement God's Word in our lives.

Men, this starts with our own walk and obedience to God. With God's Spirit, we need to engage ourselves in studying, meditating, and obeying the Word of God. Above all, we need to show our wives, *by example*, how to be filled with God's Spirit in order to be different. When our wives have flaws in their character, we know what to do to influence them to change. The spirituality of our wives is a reflection of our own walk with God, because they are our glory!

Think about that. Jesus is the head of every man, right? A man is the head of his wife. Who is the leader of every man? Jesus is. Where does every man get his teachings in order to lead his wife? It should be from Jesus. Now, who is the head of the wife? Her husband is. So who is responsible to pass on the teachings of Jesus to her? Most likely her husband, since he is her head! A husband must set apart his wife through modeling and teaching the doctrines of Jesus. Paul says, "But there is one thing I want you to know: The head of every man is Christ, the head of woman is man, and the head of Christ is God" (1 Corinthians 11:3).

In Paul's day, some women had a destructive behavior during the worship services at the church of Corinth. In order to maintain order and avoid confusion, Paul instructed the Corinthian wives not to become a distraction during the worship setting. If they had any questions, they should ask their own husbands at home (1 Corinthians 14:33–34). Now, don't misunderstand that passage. It does not mean that women should never ask questions in a public setting. Jesus communicated and discussed spiritual matters with women during his earthly ministry. Both Christian men and women have the Holy Spirit living in them. They are both called to teach and preach the kingdom of God. Rather, Paul's goal was to avoid confusion (verse 33). He was concerned about showing proper respect when Christians meet together (verse 40).

But notice something important: the fact that women were instructed to ask their husbands biblical questions means they had husbands who knew God's Word. It also means God expects Bible study at home between husbands and wives. He wants fathers and mothers to have Bible studies at home for their families as well; otherwise, he would not have required parents to teach their children (Deuteronomy 6, Proverbs 22:6).

Unfortunately, some of us have failed to be pastors to our wives. We rely on a pastor or the spiritual leaders of a local church to do our job. A local church can, and should, assist in discipling our families, but the local church is not a replacement for what we should do for our own wives at home. Since they are *our* wives, we are responsible to take care of them in all aspects of life, both spiritual and physical. Does that mean a wife should not privately study God's Word? Of course not! She is responsible to study and obey Jesus's doctrines just like her husband. But there is power in a team. When we know God and share God with our wives, we will both reap the benefits. If we fail, our wives will be our helpers to bring us back to God. If they fail, we can help bring them back. Sharing God's Word with our wives is good for our marriage. When our wives know the Scripture, they will be good helpers to us when we struggle in our relationship with God. We must be the leader in teaching God's Word to our spouse, and we must set the spiritual tone of our marriages. When we and our wives know God, we will work together to glorify God.

There is another way to "sanctify" or "set apart" our wives. That is to prefer our wife above all other women. Everyone should know which women are our wives! The husband presents his wife to the world as the preferred woman he chose among all women to be his wife. She is more qualified, beautiful, and useful to him than all other women. He selected her as the best player to play the game of life with him, and he's clearly proud of her!

Understanding Our Wives

As the savior of his wife, the husband needs to know his wife well enough to be able to save her. The Bible commands the husband to live with his wife according to understanding (1 Peter 3:7). This means knowing our wives well, being well aware of both their strengths and their flaws. The flaws that a husband discovers in the character of his wife are not to be used to make a public display or take up a judgmental attitude toward her, but to help him point her to Christ.

Jesus knew our problems before he died for us. Likewise, a husband must be willing to die in order to save his wife. The husband is to apply the knowledge he has about his wife for the best interest of the relationship. He has to follow the example of his head, Jesus Christ, to make good use of what he knows about his wife, making decisions that glorify God.

Because he is her earthly savior, a husband's primary focus should be the welfare of his wife. The husband should man up to save his wife's reputation when other people are speaking evil about her or when other threats come into her life.

I asked my sister Linda (who is single at the time of this writing) this question: "How would you want your husband to be your savior?"

She replied: "As a woman I feel that a man should always be sure to make me feel safe and secure. Just sometimes? No! Almost all the time, women feel the need to have someone who can rescue them in all situations, regardless if I am in the wrong or in the right. If I am in the wrong, he can deal with me later in private. But to have someone stand up for me is awesome. He should provide for me in many ways—emotionally is one of the biggest ways men and women think differently. I like it when a man listens to me and asks questions that show me he is listening to me. It doesn't matter if it is about the stupidest thing or the most profound thought that only God can comprehend—I like to know he is listening.

"I think husbands should have frequent days where they experience what it's like to be a wife, or better yet a mother (I hope to be one someday, God willing). I also believe it is important for a husband to remember on a daily basis how to be a friend to his wife. After all, I would hope that friendship is the reason married couples became an 'item.' At the end of a hard, long day of work, I would want to chill with my best friend, knowing he would listen to me and talk to me about my day. As my companion, he would know how to help me not think of what was so frustrating. To me the greatest thing I have heard about having a husband for a friend is that you can cry on his shoulder and fall asleep in the same bed and wake up the next morning and not have to run away thinking you're going to get in trouble."

Most women can identify with Linda. Thank you, my sister! May your future husband be your friend and savior!

As the savior of his wife, the husband must secure his wife, or put her in a safe place or environment. He must understand her well enough to provide for her appropriately. On a very practical level, the husband needs to consider whether the environment in which he wants to dwell is safe to live in with his queen.

The husband must also secure his relationship with his wife. And there is only one truly safe place he can do that. We secure our money in the bank. The heart of the husband is the bank in which he must secure his wife. His heart must have room only for his wife. After God, nothing must be considered more important to a husband than his wife. His wife is his special treasure, which needs to be secured. That is why, as her savior, the husband must ensure that his wife knows she is safe in the relationship. The husband is the safety of his wife. Tell your wife this: "Honey, you are safe because I am your savior. My heart is for you and you alone, my darling. All I want is to protect you. I am your protection because I am your husband. I will continue protecting you as long as God is my Protector."

According to God, man is the head and the savior of his wife. Let us live like that is true!

SERVING OUR WIVES

"The greatest among you must be a servant.
But those who exalt themselves will be humbled, and those
who humble themselves will be exalted."
—MATTHEW 23:11–12

Most men think they are the greatest in their families. Yet many fail to fulfill the basic requirement of greatness, which is to be a servant. Our wives will understand and appreciate the position of leadership God has entrusted to us in the family when our words and actions turn into loving acts of service to them and to our children. Our goal as husbands is to be like our Lord Jesus Christ, serving our wives like he serves the church, his bride.

Husbands are not the kings of the house, but servants. God has placed us in a position of leadership in our marriages in order to serve our wives. I serve my employer in order to provide for the needs of my wife. But I serve my wife because I love her and because my Lord Jesus commands me to serve her. If the need for money makes me mop the floor of the company I work for, then love for my wife makes me do it at home. If money makes me a dishwasher at work, love for my wife makes me wash the dishes at home. At the restaurant where I used to work, I cooked for people so that I could receive a paycheck every Friday. I experience greater satisfaction in cooking for my sweetie. Serving my wife gives me joy because it gives her time to relax and enjoy herself. My wife has no one in the world to serve her freely but me, because she is my wife. My acts of service to my wife show her that I am a real disciple of Jesus. She loves Jesus more than she does me because *he* gave me to her in order to illustrate his attitude of servanthood to the world. As a husband, I only have one person to serve. That is my wife. As a Christian *man*, I serve the world; as a *husband*, I serve my wife.

Jesus, the Son of God, left heaven—to come to earth . . . to do what? He came to serve mankind! As the King of Kings, Jesus is worthy to be served. Yet he chose to be the servant of the world. Through the acts of service Jesus offered during his earthly ministry and through his ongoing service to us as the resurrected Christ, he imparts to the people who trust him the qualities required to become servants of God. He taught us that greatness is serving other people, not for vain and personal ambition or to dominate others, but for God's glory and their benefit. Jesus said, "You call Me 'Teacher' and 'Lord,' and you are right, because that's what I am. And since I, your Lord and Teacher, have washed your feet, you ought to wash each other's feet. I have given you an example to follow. Do as I have done to you. I tell you the truth, slaves are not greater than their master. Nor is the messenger more important than the one who sends the message. Now that you know these things, God will bless you for doing them" (John 13:13–17). In other words, Jesus our Lord serves us so we can become servants to other people.

Let's bring this down into practical terms. In most homes in the world, the wives do the majority of housework—if not all of it—without any help from their husbands, whom God calls to serve their wives like Jesus serves the world. The workload in the house can put extreme pressure on wives, which often leads to frustration, loneliness, depression, disinterest in making love, and various kinds of distress. Unfortunately, when a wife seeks support from a man who does not understand what it means to be a husband to her, "it is likely to be interpreted as nagging, complaining, self-pity, and eye-gouging hostility of various forms."[7] Society expects a lot of women to do all the household responsibilities, as though marriage is designed for one person. But the Bible says, "Two people are better off than one, for they can help each other succeed" (Ecclesiastes 4:9).

A husband needs to work together with his wife for the betterment of their marriage. He also needs to pray for her. Husbands need to understand that "sometimes your wife may feel the pressure of so many expectations at once that it overwhelms her, and this makes her less effective in getting done what she needs to do. She may even get discouraged and short-circuit. Understanding all this will help you pray for her."[8] God often opens the spiritual eyes of a husband to see how to help his wife in the family when he starts praying for her.

It is deeply unfortunate that some husbands are actively committed to building the companies of their employers while being passive and careless about the work that needs to be done in their own marriages and homes. It is beyond my understanding to comprehend why a husband is eager to help the family of his employer by doing the work assigned to him while simultaneously destroying his own marriage because of his refusal to work together with his wife at home to glorify God. *We need to serve our wives and our families before we serve the world.*

Jesus serves us to make us his disciples, and we become husbands in order to live as servants to our wives. Like Jesus, who left heaven to become a servant of God to us, we who are disciples of Jesus leave our parents or our bachelor lifestyles to give exclusive and first-class service to our wives whom we love. Jesus makes it clear why he comes into our lives: "For even the Son of Man came not to be served but to serve others and to give His life as a ransom for many" (Matthew 20:28).

Becoming a Servant

The word *servant* in Greek is διακονέω, *diakoneo*, which has different meanings. In order for a husband to be a Christlike servant, he must understand both what it means to be a servant and the needs of the person who needs his service.

Using *The Theological Dictionary of the New Testament,* I will point out different aspects of what it means for a husband to be a servant to his wife:

First, to be a servant husband means "to wait at a table and offer food and drink to the guests." A wife is the special guest of her husband. Knowing his role as her servant, the husband waits at the table of his house to offer food and drink. He cooks and supplies food—the basic need of life—to his wife. A loving husband will prepare food for his wife because she is his queen, his first lady. As a servant, the husband waits at the door of his house to remove the shoes from the feet of his wife and wash her feet.

Second, to be a servant husband means "to attend to anything that may serve [your wife's] interests." Jesus set his interests as the Son of God aside to serve God's interests to save us. "Though He was God, He did not think of equality with God as something to cling to. Instead, He gave up His divine privileges; He took the humble position of a slave and was born as a human being. When He appeared in human form, He humbled Himself in obedience to God and died a criminal's death on a cross" (Philippians 2:6–8). Jesus put obedience and honoring his Father above all. A husband who is following Jesus will consider the interests and needs of his wife before his own. In practical terms, this may look like sharing the workload at home. I share the workload in taking care of the children and domestic work. My love for my wife will not let me stay on the sidelines while she is doing everything in the house. Because I am her husband, I must work together with my wife to get the domestic work done. When we are working outside the house, our wives may not see what we are doing as contributing to the household. So if we are to be successful at husbanding, we must take their perspective of working and helping in our homes into account. It is useless to argue that we have already worked enough today—use the same energy you would spend arguing to pick up a dishcloth and start drying.[9] God's righteousness in our hearts will compel us to share the load of the household.

Third, to be a servant husband means "to take care of the poor and the sick." Jesus took care of the poor and healed the sick. Marital relationships may suffer misfortunes such as unexpected sickness and financial turmoil. When these problems hit, the husband must be like Jesus in taking care of his wife for God's glory. The time of sickness and need is not the time for a husband to abandon his wife, but the time to model the love of Christ to her by providing comfort and the things necessary to sustain life.

Fourth, to be a servant husband means "to be a slave." A master-slave type of relationship depicts the idea of belonging and ownership. The slave belongs to his master. Jesus is our Lord because he bought us with his blood. Therefore, we belong to him. That is why Christians must glorify God with their bodies and spirits (1 Corinthians 6:19–20). The wife is the glory of the husband; therefore, a wife has exclusive rights to everything her husband has and does. A wife feels secure when she knows that her husband belongs to her only. The husband should give no other woman the marital rights that are reserved exclusively for his wife. As a husband, I know and accept this: *I am a slave to my wife to meet her needs for the glory of God.*

Meeting Her Needs

As we have stated before, the husband must understand the needs of his wife. A husband can serve his wife well only if he knows her needs. A husband must live with his wife according to understanding in order to know her needs and be a good servant to her. We read in 1 Peter 3:7 these comforting and inspired words: "In the same way, you husbands must give honor to your wives. Treat your wife with understanding as you live together. She may be weaker than you are, but she is your equal partner in God's gift of new life. Treat her as you should so your prayers will not be hindered."

A woman who becomes a wife has needs that a husband must understand and meet one by one. These include emotional, physical, and spiritual needs. With God's Word and Spirit, a husband should be well-equipped to satisfy the needs of his wife. The husband needs to attach to his wife emotionally by spending time with her and listening attentively to her thoughts and feelings. This will create intimacy. After all, the husband chose his wife to *be with her,* like Jesus chose his disciples to be with them (Mark 4:13–14).

One of the physical needs of a wife is for sexual intercourse. When the emotional needs of a wife are met effectively so that lasting intimacy is formed, she will long to have sex with her husband. This is according to God's design. He wants the husband to leave his parents to become one flesh physically with his wife only (Genesis 2:24). To meet the physical and emotional needs of his wife, the husband needs to use his mouth and speak to his wife with words that express his unconditional love for her. He needs to use his hands to hold and bless her, his lips to kiss her, and his feet to take a romantic walk and exercise with her. Finally, the wife must know by commitment and experience that her husband's body is hers to enjoy sexual intercourse.

Wives also have spiritual needs. Since females are made in the image of God, they need to be connected with God through their spirits in order to become godly wives to their husbands. The husband is God's chosen instrument to lead his wife to the Lord. He must study and obey God's Word before his wife. God's Spirit will use the husband's godly lifestyle to stir up the heart of the wife to serve Jesus. The husband must study the Bible with his wife and encourage her to do personal study also. He should pray with and for his wife. He should serve God together with his wife so they can remain spiritually stable as a couple.

If a husband does not know the needs of his wife, he must simply ask, and she will tell him. Only when we know a need can we serve effectively. We need to regularly talk with our wives and constantly pray to our heavenly Father so that we can know and meet the needs of our beloved spouses. Remember that God chose us to be the leaders, providers, and protectors in our marriages. Thus we truly do become the greatest in the family in function. We are to be servants in marriage for God. And he will reward us—not only during our journey on earth with our wives, but also when we meet him in glory. Loving our wives like Jesus loves us will help us to become servants. This is our message for the world and our local church: "I am a servant of God to serve my wife because I want to be like Christ Jesus."

If we fail to become servants to our wives, they will be overwhelmed in the marriage with the cares of life, and you can bet Satan will advise them to move on with their lives! When we don't serve our wives, we sin against God, and we make our wives vulnerable. We cannot be so busy working for the world that we neglect our marital household obligations. As men, we work outside the home to provide for our wives. As husbands, we work inside the home to make our wives live comfortably and happily.

We become husbands when we leave our old lifestyles to serve our wives like Jesus who left heaven and came to earth so he could serve us. We do not come into marriage relationships for vain and personal ambition so that we can dominate our wives, but so that we can be their loving servants. As obedient children, our heavenly Father expects us to be godly leaders in our marriages, modeling to our wives what it means to be servants like Jesus. We did not marry our wives to change them, but to serve them for God's glory. May God help us to become husbands who serve our wives!

FOLLOWING GOD'S DESIGN FOR FAMILY

*"The Lord God placed the man in the Garden of Eden
to tend and watch over it."*
—GENESIS 2:15

*"God puts the responsibility to love primarily on the husbands:
For husbands, this means love your wives, just as Christ
loved the church. He gave up his life for her to make her holy
and clean, washed by the cleansing of God's word."*
—EPHESIANS 5:25–26

*"God puts the responsibility to respect primarily on the wives:
So again I say, each man must love his wife as he loves himself,
and the wife must respect her husband."*
—EPHESIANS 5:33

*"God wants children to honor and respect their parents:
Children, obey your parents because you belong to the Lord,
[a] for this is the right thing to do. "Honor your father and
mother." This is the first commandment with a promise:
If you honor your father and mother, "things will go well
for you, and you will have a long life on the earth."*
—EPHESIANS 6:1-3

Is it possible for a child conceived in rape and raised without a father to become a good husband? The answer to that question depends on who we ask. If we ask society, we might be encouraged to abort the child—we'll assume he can't overcome, and the circumstances in which he was conceived are just too awful. But if we turn to God, the answer will be yes—even a child conceived in rape can become what he ought to be with the help of God. God alone is able to turn the horrible events of life into beautiful experiences for his glory. God made this glorious universe out of nothing to reveal his nature, and he took a bad choice my father made and formed me into a wonderful creature. It is because of God's grace, and one woman's decision to blindly trust in a powerful God she did not even know at the time, that I can say that God's ways and his designs are perfect!

There is indeed a design for marriage and family. God has revealed it in the Bible, and he will help anyone to live it out if we trust him and seek his help. I owe my spiritual growth in grace and my good marital relationship with my wife to my Christian brothers and sisters who faithfully let the Holy Spirit use them to spread the message of the Scriptures. A few years after I arrived in America, I began listening to 89.3 FM WRNB, which is located in South Florida. God used their Bible-centered ministries to awaken my desire for a deeper understanding of my heavenly Father through study-ing the Scriptures with my partner, the Holy Spirit. I have since learned of the depth of reading and applying the Bible in my relationship with my wife and family. I have read the Bible forty-two times already, and I plan to continue reading it from Genesis to Revelation until I am unable to do so physically. Praise God! He deserves the glory and the honor.

Despite the current attacks on Christian values in America and the threats of undermining and changing the definition of marriage and fam-ily, God's plan will prevail, for he is the eternal, mighty God. No human civilization can stop God from accomplishing his will for humanity! It is normal for the gates of hell to bring war against the church, but no weap-ons formed against the anointed people of God shall succeed, because Jesus won the victory when he died on the cross and rose from the dead to secure his finished work (see Isaiah 54:17, Colossians 2:13–15, 1 John 5:5). "But you belong to God, my dear children. You have already won a victory over those people, because the Spirit who lives in you is greater than the spirit who lives in the world" (1 John 4:4).

Following God's design for family is good for the enhancement of his kingdom and the continuity of humanity.

God's Design for the Family

God's design for family can be described this way: *Love* (the husband) marries with *respect* (the wife) to bring forth *honor* and *respect* (the children). God made husbands to love their wives and wives to respect their husbands, and he blesses the marriage with children to honor and obey their parents. That is beautiful! We should not settle for anything less, and we must work with God to produce and preserve the marriage he wants for us.

Throughout history, God has always used marriage and family to accomplish his plans. In many ways, marriage is the hope of the world. Without the family structured as God created it from the beginning, we open the door for Satan to destroy and steal our blessings, our fellowship with God and our families, and our right as people made in God's image to govern and keep the earth for his glory.

As husbands, we dare not follow the example of Adam, who allowed Satan to damage God's design for his marriage. He made a deliberate choice to sin with his wife rather than protecting her by obeying God. Adam's disobedience brought death to every relationship in his life, both with God and others, but Jesus's obedience gives us abundant life (see Romans 5:12–21). In Jesus Christ, God empowered us with his Spirit at conversion to cultivate and keep a good marriage. In the same way that God sought out Adam to save his marriage after the enemy deceived him and his wife, God is seeking to rescue our marriages from wrong worldviews. "The eyes of the Lord search the whole earth in order to strengthen those whose hearts are fully committed to Him" (2 Chronicles 16:9).

I am so grateful to God for making me a godly husband to my wife in order to preserve his design in our family! After my salvation in Christ, it is my relationship with my wife—which exemplifies Christ's relationship with the church—that I find most fulfilling in life. I am happy to be a husband to my wife, and I thank Jesus for being my head.

I encourage all men to become the husbands God designed them to be in Christ Jesus. God's plan is always good! Good husbands become good fathers, and the combination of a good husband and a good father builds a strong and stable family for our children. God wants children to be raised in a loving environment. As husbands who love God, we must make our head, Jesus Christ, proud of us like he makes God the Father, his head, proud of him. With Jesus in us through his Spirit, we have all the resources we need to be godly husbands to our wives. Let's go, husbands!

The Power to Become

What God wants to see in our marriages is impossible to achieve through our human efforts alone. The Holy Spirit is our power to become what we are supposed to be in our relationship with our wives. Through our fellowship with him, the Holy Spirit applies God's Word to our hearts so that we may have life in order to love our wives. "The Spirit of God, who raised Jesus from the dead, lives in you. And just as God raised Christ Jesus from the dead, He will give life to your mortal bodies by this same Spirit living within you" (Romans 8:11). *The Holy Spirit can make what is true in Jesus Christ real in our lives.* Apart from the work of the Holy Spirit in us, we will never be able to live like Jesus Christ. God's Spirit is responsible to reveal God's nature through us. It is imperative that we do not allow personal fulfillments, the daily grind of living, and the circumstances of life hinder the way the Holy Spirit can work through us.

The key to shutting the door of divorce is for more husbands to have and be filled with the Holy Spirit. "Don't be drunk with wine, because that will ruin your life. Instead, be filled with the Holy Spirit, singing psalms and hymns and spiritual songs among yourselves, and making music to the Lord in your hearts. And give thanks for everything to God the Father in the name of our Lord Jesus Christ" (Ephesians 5:18–20). When we are under the influence of the Holy Spirit, we will let go of our egos so we can live for God's glory and for the good of our marriages. His controlling power will change our characters and actions, and we will no longer walk and talk like the ungodly husbands of this world. When God is running and directing our lives, our marriages will benefit, and our children will have good examples to mimic. Why are so many marriages in peril? I believe it is because we are not filled with the Holy Spirit. God's instruction on how to be filled with the Holy Spirit is given to us in Ephesians 5:19–21. The command is given in verse 18, and the results of living out a Spirit-filled experience in our marriages are laid out in verses 22–33.

We see at least three principles in verses 19–21 concerning a Spirit-filled life: *worship, thanksgiving,* and *submitting to one another.*

Worship consists of our speaking edification to one another (when we meet as a church and the way we talk in our daily conversations), singing to and for ourselves and to one another, and making melody within our hearts to the Lord. A simple definition of worship is to behold the nature of God in spirit and truth—to behold him in the truth about God and ourselves. The angels do not rest day or night, but are saying, "Holy, holy, holy, Lord God Almighty, who was and is and is to come!" (Revelation 4:8 NKJV). They are focused on who God is rather than on what he does. We worship God's nature, and we praise his actions.

David blessed the Lord because of the wonderful work God did for his soul. "Let all that I am praise the Lord; with my whole heart, I will praise his holy name. Let all that I am praise the Lord; may I never forget the good things he does for me. He forgives all my sins and heals all my diseases. He redeems me from death and crowns me with love and tender mercies. He fills my life with good things. My youth is renewed like the eagle's! The Lord gives righteousness and justice to all who are treated unfairly" (Psalm 103:1–6). The word "bless" means to "speak well of." We need to speak well of God for what he does for us.

Thanksgiving should be directed to God the Father for making us good husbands and for being a good head to us. We thank him, not only for what he does, but also for who he is.

The final aspect of being filled with God's Spirit is *submitting to one another*. This means we must stop being selfish and proud. We are all saved because of God's love, mercy, and grace. We are brothers and sisters in his family. Family members should not have any problem submitting to each other. If we seem to have an ongoing problem with that way of living, we need to question even our salvation.

Marriage is meant to be good. God designed it to glorify him through the obedience of a husband and a wife with the empowerment of his Spirit. Yet, the goodness of God in marriage cannot become a reality if a couple refuses to serve God together. "This is another way of saying that marriage is based on God's will, not just on your desires. A Christian marriage is one that belongs to Christ and in which the husband and the wife consciously seek to find out what Christ wants to do with His possession."[10]

We will follow God's design for marriage when we go back to Genesis to discover who he entrusted the earth to—the first marriage, Adam and Eve, who became a husband and a wife. Without marriage, the world cannot be preserved. God created marriage to rule over the earth through the husband and the wife, and their offspring will continue that rule through the divine design. From the beginning, God made Adam and gave him Eve to become his wife in a home called Paradise, which they were to keep and to cultivate. God's design for the world was that the marriage would be the vehicle through which his plans would be fulfilled on earth.

By his very nature, God is a God of family—he is Father, Son, and Spirit. He created the first marriage between Adam and Eve to set forth the example that all marriages should follow. Unfortunately, Satan successfully influenced the first couple to sin against God, and thus they transferred their God-given right to govern the earth to the enemy. Fortunately, God rescued them and restored order. Jesus came to bring back men and women to God, enabling them to become good husbands and wives to live for his glory.

God recreated us in Christ Jesus. He brings his redeemed sons and daughters together to create good marital relationships that aim to glorify him in how they relate to one another. God's design for the family is perfect, it is beautiful, and it should be our diligent aim.

A FINAL WORD FOR HUSBANDS

I have learned over the course of my life as a Christian that loving others is not always easy. The practice of love can be challenging, especially depending on the receptivity and attitude of the person I want to love. Yet I have to love people no matter how they decide to live their lives. *My love for people, and particularly for my wife, has nothing to do with what they say and do, but everything to do with what God has done in my heart when he poured his love into my heart through his Spirit without measure.* "And this hope will not lead to disappointment. For we know how dearly God loves us, because He has given us the Holy Spirit to fill our hearts with His love" (Romans 5:5). My heart fills with love because of the indwelling presence of God's Spirit. Amen to that!

There are three biblical principles we must understand and accept about loving our wives.

The first principle is that it is hard and costly to love. We need to know that love oftentimes demands hardship and suffering. We see that in the life of Jesus. He was rejected and despised just because he loved us (Isaiah 53). We turned our back on Jesus and looked at him with disdain although he loved us. Before we understood and accepted his love, we preferred sinning to satisfy our desires. Jesus is called a "man of sorrows, acquainted with bitterest grief" (Isaiah 53:3). He willingly accepted those titles and endured the pains that came with them because he loved us.

This is personal. Most of us treated Jesus harshly for a good portion of our lives before we repented from our sins. We caused him indescribable pain before we understood his love for us. He bore our sins and interceded for us because he loved us. He was wounded and crushed for our rebellion against God. God forgave our sins because Jesus died in our place. God healed our souls from sin because Jesus became sin for us so that we could become his righteousness (Isaiah 53:8, 2 Corinthians 5:21). God blessed us with many heavenly blessings because Jesus loved us (Ephesians 1:3–14).

We mocked Jesus, called him names, and ridiculed him although he loved us. He never retaliated or thought about taking vengeance for all the sorrows and agony we caused him. We did every imaginable sin to show our unworthiness of Jesus's love. Yet he loved—and loves—us anyway. It was never easy for Jesus to love us. It cost Jesus much to love us. Jesus endured the sufferings of the cross and gladly suffered because he loved us. He wanted and still wants our salvation and the salvation of humankind. What a pure love Jesus has for us!

This same Jesus now asks me as a husband to love my wife. What do you think? If I must walk in the footsteps of Jesus to love my wife, do you think this "loving thing" will be easy? No. My wife may despise and reject me, but I must love her because I love Jesus. My wife might cause me grief, sorrows, and troubles; she might wrongly punish me; yet I must love her because I love Jesus and I want to be like him. I am grateful to God for my wife, because she does not make loving her as hard as it was for Jesus to love me! In fact, Djenny makes it easy for me to love her. I am glad that the love of God saved my wife to bless me with many blessings in Christ Jesus. But some wives can make it difficult for their husbands to love them, like it was for Jesus.

A husband needs to understand that loving his wife might require him to endure misfortunes in life. In spite of all the headaches and pains a wife can cause her husband, God commands him to love her. Difficult, right? But not impossible, because God has made it possible in Christ Jesus for a husband to love his wife as Jesus loves him!

Nor does suffering get the final word. My love for my wife can lead her to repentance, just as the love of God led me to repentance. My love for my wife can heal her, just as Jesus's love has healed my soul. My love for my wife can satisfy her needs, just as Jesus's love gratifies my needs. There is something beautiful about God's love, however humanly impossible it is to practice fully: "Love is patient and kind. Love is not jealous or boastful or proud or rude. It does not demand its own way. It is not irritable, and it keeps no record of being wronged. It does not rejoice about injustice but rejoices whenever the truth wins out. Love never gives up, never loses faith, is always hopeful, and endures through every circumstance" (1 Corinthians 13:4–7). That is the type of love God wants for marriage. No marriage will fail to accomplish God's purposes if love is its foundation. No good wife will reject the kinds of love from her husband described above.

For the sake of being loyal to Jesus, a husband must love his wife no matter what she does or says to him. A husband must choose between pleasing himself and pleasing Jesus, who loved him even to the point of death on the cross. Jesus said to his disciples, "If any of you wants to be My follower, you must turn from your selfish ways, take up your cross, and follow Me" (Matthew 16:24).

When the disciples heard what Jesus said about the lifelong responsibility of a husband to his wife, they said to him, "Then it is better not to marry! Not everyone can accept this statement." Jesus then said, "Only those whom God helps. Some are born as eunuchs, some have been made eunuchs by others, and some choose not to marry for the sake of the Kingdom of Heaven. Let anyone accept this who can" (Matthew 19:10–12). The disciples accepted the challenge of Jesus to love their wives and be loyal to them until death. No matter how a wife chooses to live her life, the husband must remain loyal to Jesus.

The second principle is that this type of love is unbreakable. The love we receive from God to give to our wives has no end. This unbreakable love for our wives is illustrated in the connection of the members of the human body. Every member of the body connects to the others, and their connection is unbreakable. We are called to love our wives as our own bodies (Ephesians 5:28–30). As the Scriptures say, "Therefore a man shall leave his father and mother and be joined to his wife, and they shall become one flesh" (Genesis 2:24 NKJV). Because we love our wives, we cleave to them in order to become one flesh. We are connected to our wives as body parts are connected to each other. If we think about withdrawing our love from our wives, we are basically thinking about tearing our own bodies apart. Think about the agony and pain we would face if our bodies were torn apart! The same degree of pain will be faced in marriage if we choose not to love our wives. Great are the agony, suffering, and sorrows that characterize most marriages in our generation because of the absence of the love of the husband for his wife. If we allow worldly pleasures to keep us from loving our wives, our very own wives will become the source of our own misery and grief.

The ideal plan of God for a husband is to leave all to cleave to his wife in order to demonstrate his ultimate, unbreakable love for her. Nothing and no one should dismantle the love that unites the husband to his wife to glorify God as one. Materialism, worldly pleasures, parents, position, privileges, fame, and misfortunes should not destroy the love of the husband for his wife. Nothing, absolutely *nothing*, should separate the wife from the love of her husband, because God who is love lives in the heart of the husband. Nothing can separate the husband from the love of God because of what Jesus has done for him (Romans 8:31–39). Likewise, nothing should stop the husband from loving his wife. Since God's love for the husband is unbreakable, his love for his wife is unbreakable also. The husband gives to his wife the same love that he receives from God. He receives unbreakable love from God, and therefore he loves his wife with unbreakable love.

What God asks of us, he provides us with the means to do. Jesus Christ is the only means available to us to love God and our wives. Without Jesus in our hearts, we will have no real love in our hearts. With Jesus in our hearts through the indwelling presence of his Spirit, love becomes real in our way of living.

The third principle a husband needs to understand and accept is that the kind of love God wants him to have toward his wife is preactivated in Christ Jesus and ready to use immediately. The code to activate the love of God in the heart of a husband is the Holy Spirit. At conversion, God did something wonderful for every disciple of Jesus: he shared his loving nature with us so that we might live like his children (2 Peter 4:3–10). *The wonders of God's love are in the heart of every follower of Jesus.* What a husband who is a follower of Jesus must do to love his wife is to activate God's love in his heart and use it immediately in his relationship with her.

There is no activation fee for love. Jesus already paid the price in full at Calvary. There is no annual fee to pay. Jesus died once for all. To activate love in his heart, a husband must surrender his will and desires to the Holy Spirit who dwells in him. Once he makes that decision, he must prove the veracity of his choice through daily study of the Bible and a constant prayer life with the help of God's Spirit.

The ultimate choice a husband has to make is this: who is in charge? Me or God's Spirit? My desires or the desires of God's Spirit? If a husband chooses to live according to his desires, he will eventually hate his wife. But if he chooses to live according to the desires of God's Spirit, he will certainly love his wife. Love is one of many qualities the Holy Spirit desires to produce through the husband for his wife. Study Galatians 5:16–24 to discover the outcome of a life that is controlled by the Holy Spirit compared to a life that is controlled by the passions and desires of the sinful nature.

Blessed are the husbands whose wives are easy to love! But blessed too are the husbands whose wives are difficult, for the Holy Spirit will make it possible and even easy for them to love their wives, and they will grow in the fruits of the Spirit and the nature of God. I choose to live according to the Holy Spirit so that I can love my wife for God's glory. What is your choice?

"But if you refuse to serve the Lord, then choose today whom you will serve. Would you prefer the gods your ancestors served beyond the Euphrates? Or will it be the gods of the Amorites in whose land you now live? But as for me and my family, we will serve the Lord" (Joshua 24:15). We can become the husbands God wants us to be by being filled with the Holy Spirit.

PART II
THE WIFE

God made women with the potential of becoming wives. Most women have big dreams for their marriages and desire to succeed in their marital journey. Some of these women are well educated, wealthy, and even well known in their communities and around the world. Yet, the ideal marriage relationship they foresaw while growing up has not materialized. Some opt for divorce because of marital challenges, and others choose to remain married under difficult circumstances. Some want to know why their marriages are not working, and they look for help to change their marital misfortunes into blessings. This book is written especially to help women who are getting ready for marriage and those who are already married and are struggling—who want to know what it means to become a godly wife.

Just like a man doesn't become a true husband just by handing over a ring, a woman doesn't become a true wife just because she says "I do" and kisses her man at the altar. We strongly believe that the primary reason so many married couples struggle to live joyfully with one another is lack of knowledge. Many women get married without the proper training and understanding of how to become godly wives to their husbands. If a woman does not know what it means to become a godly wife, she will not be able to function well within the marriage or relate to her husband properly. As a woman who loves God, it is important for you to learn how to become a wife. We have written this book to share biblical teachings that will equip women to become godly wives to their husbands. It is our heartfelt desire that husbands and wives enjoy the good marriage God created for them.

God has established marriage as an institution, and every person must learn from the school of marriage—through the Scriptures, through premarital counseling, and we hope through this book—to know what their marriage careers will entail. Just as God created males to become husbands for life, God created females to have a lifetime career called "wife and mother." Every woman who marries must let God teach her how to become a wife and a mother in the truest sense.

This book so far has been written from Frantz's perspective. At this point, we will switch to Djenny's. The first part of our journey with you, the reader, has come to a close. Now it's time to adventure into the second.

SUPPORTING OUR HUSBANDS

"Then the Lord God said, 'It is not good for the man
to be alone. I will make a helper who is just right for him.'"
—GENESIS 2:18

I n the brightest and in the darkest moments, my support for my husband is unwavering. As his wife, I am his number-one supporter. I love being married because it is so great to share life with my husband, to complete him. Supporting my husband involved seeing the gifts that God gave him so that I can assist him developing and deploying these spiritual gifts. I know my husband has talents that require my support to inspire him to put them to use, and I am doing just that. In his role as a husband, I support him to love me as he should. In his role as a pastor, I support him to be the loving and compassionate shepherd God wants him to be to his redeemed people. I support him to go back to school to get a dual master's in mental health and marriage and family therapy. I am encouraging him to get his PhD in counseling psychology because I believe that my husband's success is mine as well. As a wife, God empowers me to support my husband to reach the fullest potential of the godly man he has created him to be.

In most cases, a wife's support of her husband will determine how long they stay together and how successful their marriage can be. When sin entered into the human race due to the disobedience of the first couple, life became difficult. Many are the challenges we have to overcome in order to build healthy marital relationships! As we've read, God has placed husbands in the family to be leaders. And he has created us, their wives, to support them in accomplishing his plans for the family so that the ride of life together can be smoother. If our marriage is to last until death parts us, our supportive and cooperative role will be an important factor in making that happen. Living together in marriage cannot be what God envisioned it to be in eternity without wives being the substructures that hold the marriage together against the shocks and rough roads of life. God wants us and our husbands to be one organism. Disunity is one of the weapons Satan will use to take away the privilege of modeling the goodness of God in our marriages.

One of the meanings of the word *helper* in Genesis 2:18 is "to support." We truly become wives when we support our husbands in accomplishing the mission that God has set for our marriage. *This mission is to glorify God.* He gave the husband the leadership role to equip his family in glorifying God, and the wife is to support her husband in filling that divine purpose. Ladies, our marriages are bigger than just our desires and needs! God establishes the mission for the family, the husband implements the mission in the marriage, and the wife submits or supports her husband as he obeys and applies God's mission. There should be no fight between the husband and the wife when it comes to fulfilling God's will for their marriage. They must accept their respective roles to please God. God did not create the wife to support or submit to the mission of the husband, but to *God's* mission as it is revealed in the Bible. Both are created to be servants of God, and together they should serve their Creator.

The greatest supporter of the husband is his wife. It is right to support the man we have chosen to be our husband! After all, we selected him from among other men whom we judged unqualified to become our husband. We respected him more than the other men who wanted to go out with us. That is why we fell in love with and married him. We had the option of saying no during the courtship, but we said yes, and now it's our responsibility to support the man we chose.

When you think about it, it's strange that so many women do not want to support their husbands in marriage. Would we do this in other areas of life? Any woman who opens a business should be the first one to support it. She cannot expect other people to be the first or most passionate supporters. The support of others will come later along the way. The primary support must come from the initiator of the business. It is mind-boggling to understand why some women do not want to support the very men they chose to become their husbands, yet it seems to be the normal way of living for many wives. Such a choice will produce tensions in the marriage relationship and diminish the level of the intimacy that is possible between you.

Supporting Our Husbands in Love

Supporting our husbands entails becoming their cheerleaders and encouragers. You, the wife, are the inspirational person who keeps your husband going and gives him confidence in being the husband God wants for your marriage.

Every worthwhile thing is motivated by love. Marriage is no exception! The love we felt during the courtship period and our love for God motivate us to be committed to supporting our husbands. It was romantic and beautiful when we introduced our man to our parents, brothers, sisters, and friends, and we could not wait for the wedding ceremony to take place and to behold our groom's presence in anticipation of experiencing and exploring him in a deeper level after the ceremony was over. We invited parents, relatives, friends, and coworkers to witness our wedding ceremony, where we would promise our support to our husbands. We need to tap into that same love day by day as we make an effort to support our husbands. The desire to fight our husbands is sometimes real in our hearts, but we did not choose our men to engage ourselves with them in strife. We planned to lovingly support them as wives who fear God. God would not ask us to support our husbands if he knew it would not be good for our relationships. So we trust God to make us what he wants us to be in our marriage relationship. We thank God for his Spirit, who enables us to be godly wives!

As women, living in a peaceful and loving environment with our husbands is one of many goals we cherish in our hearts. We can contribute to this goal by honoring our choice of a husband and keeping the promise we made before God and witnesses to sustain him. Yet our role of supporting and sustaining will not be possible independent of our relationship with God. Our support of our husbands should be rooted in our love for them, but first, it must be rooted in our love for God and our daily relationship with him. We trust him to help us be godly wives and to protect our marriages from evil. What a joy for a wife to be used by God to lift her husband up!

God makes marriage, and Jesus is the means to successful marriages. He designs the strategy of the game of life and calls the plays. He instructs our husbands, who are the leaders of our marriages, in how to lead. Our husbands guide us in doing God's will to glorify him.

If we choose not to follow the lead of our husbands, our marriages will lose their godly identity. Satan and his demons know how to bring disunity in our marriages to mess up God's plan. The enemy caused the first couple, Adam and Eve, to rebel against God. He's still up to his old tricks! Our marriages are not exempt from his attacks, but with God's Spirit living in us, we can be assured that no evil will conquer our marriages. Ladies, we don't want to follow in Eve's footsteps and carry on conversations with Satan that end in our obeying him. We choose rather to communicate with God and our husbands to know what needs to be done for the family. Adam was made first and Eve second. Yet both needed each other to live for God. We also must work together with God and our husbands to build stable and strong marriages for others to mimic.

Support and Submission

Supporting our husbands includes being submissive to our husbands. God instructs and blesses our husbands to love us as Jesus loves the church. "Wives, submit to your own husbands, as to the Lord" (Ephesians 5:22). Jesus also asks *us* to submit to our own husbands for God's glory. The word "own" in Ephesians 5:22 give us the impression that the wives to whom Paul was speaking had no problem submitting their lives to other men, but they found it hard to submit to their own husbands. To resolve this problem, Paul reminded those wives of God's heart for them in regard to their relationships with their husbands.

Some of us are kind to other men, but we treat our own husbands like they are nothing. Some of us give our best for our employers, but we disdain our own husbands when they ask things of us. Is it wise to build up our employers' companies and marriages through our submission to them while we refuse to submit our lives to our husbands to construct our own marriages and households? That is not God's plan for us. If we're not careful, we may even let the devil deceive us into submitting ourselves to other men who want to exploit our beauty and sexuality, which are reserved exclusively for our husbands. We should not be naïve to ignore the fact that some men out there want to destroy our marriages. Submitting ourselves to our own husbands under God's blessing will protect us from such threats and allow us to enjoy each other.

Some wives have no problem being submissive to their male supervisors at work, perhaps because they want a paycheck or because they like to serve customers. They have no problem submitting their lives to a boss even though they may not like him. However, they find it hard to submit to their husbands once they're at home. They justify their rebellious behavior toward their husbands on the basis that their husbands are not the type of husbands God expects them to be! Ladies, that might be true. Your husband might not be what God wants him to be. But for us to respond with rebellion is the wrong answer. This is the time when we must be on our husband's side to help him become a godly husband. We must pray for him, submit to him, and support him, and let God restore his soul with his love and mercy. We just need to be the wives God wants us to be.

Each one of us will stand before God alone to give account for our lives. God will give each person according to his or her own deeds. Don't be among those wives who are more concerned about keeping their jobs than saving their marriage relationships.

"Submission" can be a scary word, but it does not need to be. It's actually a principle of life that we live by all the time. When we are sick, we submit our bodies—even our lives—to doctors with no hesitation. We trust them with our lives without being concerned much about their character and conduct because becoming healthy is our priority. We receive their prescriptions with great confidence, thinking that if we follow their instructions faithfully, we will be whole. That is submission! So if we believe marriage is God's idea, and if we prioritize our marriages in our lives, should we object to submitting to our own husbands? Absolutely not! Submission is not a fearful thing, but a normal way to achieve a good, healthy result.

Submission to our husbands implies honoring and following them as they follow our Lord Jesus Christ. Since they are our head and we are their body, we need to work together to sustain our marriages. The human body illustrates how this works: the head and the body submit to each other for the welfare of the whole. If the body does not follow the head, there will be no life in it. If the head tries to charge off without the body, it will get nowhere! The head and body need to stay together and share the same vision.

Jesus is the head of his body, the church. As the body, the church is called to submit to Jesus. As discussed in the first part of this book, one of the responsibilities of our husbands is to love us with a tender and faithful affection. Christ's love for the church is the perfect example: it is sincere, pure, and constant in spite of the church's sin, failures, and imperfections. It will not be easy to submit to our husbands if they do not love us as Christ loves the church. However, we need to be careful that we do not allow the behavior of our husbands to determine whether or not we obey God. Ultimately, it is God who holds us accountable. With God's help, we can do what he expects from us if we work with him.

Some husbands misunderstand what it means for their wives to be submissive to them. They think that since they are the leaders, they can rule over their wives. They wrongly believe that the leadership role in the family demands that their wives must simply follow them. Such a forceful request is not Christlike. So what do we do if our husbands have a wrong view of submission? Obviously we don't need to adopt the same beliefs about it! However, we need to avoid engaging in a fight. We need to respectfully discuss it with them and study the Bible together on this topic.

Jesus Christ is the perfect example of what submission is all about. A worldly understanding of submission will hurt our marriage. A Christian marriage is not a place where the husband leads and we follow blindly. It is not our husbands first and us second. God designed marriage to function as a team in which we and our husbands walk side by side to reveal God to each other and to the world.

God took the rib of Adam to make Eve to become his wife. The rib is on his side and not in his back. We walked side by side with our husbands during and after the wedding ceremony, and we sat side by side on the way to our honeymoon. When we start living together, we must still live side by side to glorify God. We are equally important, because God made us both in his image. There should be no competition in the family of God. Instead, we must complete one another. God did not turn men into husbands to seek dominance over us, but to love us like Christ loves them. God wants us to agree wholeheartedly with each other, loving one another and working together with one mind and purpose. God wants both to submit to one another in accomplishing their respective roles to glorify him. "And further, submit to one another out of reverence for Christ" (Ephesians 5:21).

What then does it mean to submit to our husbands? To understand the word *submission*, let's examine its two parts. The prefix, *sub*, means "under," and the word *mission* means "a specific task with which a person or group is charged." Therefore, the word *submission* means to put under or be subject to somebody else's mission. The mission in this case is to glorify God through our marriage. Submission is a voluntary attitude wherein we choose to let go of our rights in order to live for our responsabilities to God. For example, when we are driving, we may have the right to proceed first according to the rules, but sometimes we willingly yield to let someone else go first—perhaps out of generosity or thoughtfulness to avoid an accident.

Ladies, we are better off submitting ourselves to our own husbands in order to experience God's blessings, even when it's difficult for us or when it involves laying down our rights, than allowing Satan to bring an accident into our marital relationship that can be fatal. Once an infraction is committed in our marriage, Satan will suggest that we go downtown before a judge to file for divorce. If we go downtown, it is a guarantee that our marriage will go down all the way, because we are seeking advice from someone who did not create marriage! When our marriage is in trouble, our best and only option is to go uptown to God, who will always bring our marriage up if we trust and obey him. Since he is the maker of our marriage, he surely knows how to fix it when something goes wrong.

The act of submission ought not to be forced, but voluntary. We submit ourselves to our husbands because we love them and want God's plan for our families to be done. God's purpose for us is to voluntarily submit to our husbands simply because we love and respect them. The Bible says in Ephesians 5:22, "Wives, submit yourselves to your own husbands, as to the Lord."

Having said that, here is the question we need to ask ourselves and then carefully ponder our honest answer: "Is my life under the mission of God, especially in my marriage relationship?" God's mission for marriage is clearly revealed in the Bible. We submit our lives to our husbands when they are under the mission of God and when they are not under the mission of God; we submit to them anyway and pray for their repentance. God calls us both to submit ourselves to one another in the fear of the Lord so that God's purposes for our marriage may be fulfilled.

To be submissive does not mean being a doormat to our husbands to step on, but rather working together with them for God's glory. We submit to our husbands not as they necessarily want us to but as unto the Lord. The Lord himself is the boundary of mutual submission. To submit to God's mission is to respect the order and the authority of God regardless of present and past circumstances. To be submissive is to put ourselves into a state of retirement and dependence for the sake of another's mission. Are we retiring our rights so that we can take our responsibility before God to submit to our husbands? If we are living to defend our rights, it is a guarantee that our marriage will suffer and may even collapse.

Our husbands can experience transformation if we let God help us to submit to them. Again, submissiveness does not mean that we are inferior to our husbands or that we are their slaves to be treated unfairly. The Bible says we become one flesh in marriage. How can one part of one's flesh be inferior? This is not possible. Jesus submits himself to God, the Father, but he is in no way inferior to him. Although Jesus was God, he made himself of no reputation, and he humbled himself and became obedient to the point of death (Philippians 2:5–11). Through the wife, God wants to teach the husband what it means to be submissive to him. Likewise, God commissions the husband to exemplify his love toward his wife so that she can effectively learn how to love the Lord. All the duties of marriage are to be performed in unity and love.

According to God's divine plan, our husbands are the head, and we are the body. Without our submission, our heads will not function properly. We did not marry our husbands to dominate them or give them orders, but to honor and support them in submission as we respectfully share our opinions and follow their lead.

Of course, ultimately we submit to our husbands out of obedience to God our Father. Is it good to obey the Lord God our Father? Of course the answer is yes, because he loves us and wants us to experience abundant life in Christ Jesus. We don't need to be afraid to obey him! If our husbands fail, should we continue doing what God wants? Yes, we should. *We do not submit to our husbands for what they do, but because we want to please God.* Do two wrongs make a right? No, they do not. Therefore, we cannot let the negative conduct of our husbands dictate *our* conduct. As daughters of God, we are led by the Holy Spirit (Romans 8:14). The right to tell us how to conduct ourselves belongs to God and to God alone. Does God command us to obey him on the basis of what other people do, or on the basis of what he did for us in Christ Jesus? We obey God because we love and trust him. That is the foundation of our submission, the foundation of our marriages, and the foundation of our entire lives.

God makes us good through Christ Jesus because he loves us. That same principle of love also works in our relationships. We do good for our husbands on the basis of our love for them. God never makes mistakes. He wants what is best for us. He would not ask our husbands to love us if he knew that wouldn't be good to accomplish his purpose in our marriages. He likewise would not ask us to submit to our husbands if he knew that it wouldn't be good to do so, that it wouldn't create intimacy in our relationship with them.

Finding Our Foundation in God

We do not own our thoughts and ideas. *We either adopt God's ideas or Satan's ideas.* We had better be careful to discern the source of ideas before we accept them as our own! Everything good comes from God, and everything that is not good does not come from him. We need to make sure that we are living out of a foundation in the character and commandments of God.

The opposite of love is hatred. If our husbands do not love us, they did not learn this behavior from God. God is love, and he shares his love with his children. Our husbands cannot love us if they are not born into the family of God, and likewise, we cannot submit to our husbands if we do not belong to God.

Once we know that we do belong to God through salvation and regeneration in Christ, we must be careful not to conform ourselves to the principles of this world—namely, their corrupted views about marriage (Romans 12:1). Rejecting a Christian, theistic worldview about marriage will lead to our rebellion against our husbands, and thus we will obey Satan. Remember, he is the source of all rebellion! He caused Eve to rebel against God, and she suggested to her husband that he do likewise. Consequently, the whole world suffers for their sin against God.

If we are in a marriage relationship where our husbands are not obeying God, we need to remember that Jesus is our Redeemer. If we do what we should—what God expects of us—we will surely be at peace. Coming to the Lord God with our concerns is exactly what he wants us to do when our husbands are not behaving in a godly manner. "Give all your worries and cares to God, for he cares about you" (1 Peter 5:7).

Our godly character and conduct can lead our husbands to Christ to receive a new heart from God so that they can love us as they should. "Wives, likewise, be submissive to your own husbands, that even if some do not obey the word, they, without a word, may be won by the conduct of their wives, when they observe your chaste conduct accompanied by fear" (1 Peter 3:1–2 NKJV). As we live a Spirit-filled life, we may win our husbands over to the Lord. Yelling at our husbands or nagging them with unedifying words will only make things worse. Thus, we will hinder the progress of our own marriage.

When we trust and obey God as the foundation of our actions and attitudes, he will be on our side to help us be victorious when we face difficulty in our marriages. If God is for us, who can be against us (Romans 8:28–31)? However, if God is not for us, all hell will break loose against us. If we have shown disrespect to our husbands, we need to confess our sins to God and seek the forgiveness of our husbands. We are their wives. God wants us to submit to the leadership of our husbands without compromising our loyalty to God. Don't use the sins that your husband commits against you to punish him. We should rather become a support for our men, and we should in humility seek to restore their fellowship with God. Love supports all (1 Corinthians 13:7).

As we read many times in the opening half of this book, God poured his love into our hearts at conversion through his Spirit so that we might love him and others (Romans 5:5). His Spirit in us produces his character in our way of living (Galatians 5:22–25). We are supposed to be led and guided by the Spirit as God's children (Romans 8:14). If we let Satan corrupt the love we have in our hearts for our husbands, he will definitely offer us an alternative. He will make us believe that another man deserves our love. We dare not fall into his temptation lest we destroy our marriages. God is bigger than the problems we are going through. He gives us grace and mercy to cope with whatever challenges life throws at us and our marriages. May the Holy Spirit enable us to lovingly submit to our husbands for God's glory!

Laying Down Our Rights

Prior to marriage, both our husbands and we forsook our rights in order to love each other. Why do we now think that if we stand for our rights in marriage, things will be better? We have to choose between these two: our rights or our God-given responsibilities. Jesus chooses to live according to God's will (John 4:34) and thus leaves us an example to follow (1 Peter 2:21). When we live for God, he will transform us from glory to glory by his Spirit (2 Corinthians 3:16–18).

Many marriages are doing badly because the husband or wife or both live only for their rights rather than for God. We will experience transformation in our families, churches, and society only when we follow the perfect example of our Lord Jesus Christ, who came not to be served but to serve. We should not live for this world, but for the world to come. We read in Romans 12:19, "'Vengeance is mine,' says the Lord."

As Christians, God did not call us to defend our rights; instead, he called us to be responsible individuals. We have the right to repay evil with evil. However, if we do that, we will be denied the privilege of doing good to overcome evil (Romans 12:21). Our responsibility is to repay evil with good deeds for God's glory. Let God defend our rights, and let us fulfill our responsibility to apply his principles in any given situation. Jesus had all the right to defend himself during his earthly ministry, but he willingly obeyed his Father's will to save humanity instead. *If Jesus had stood for his rights, none of us would have been saved.* Jesus said, "Put your sword in its place, for all who take the sword will perish by the sword. Or do you think that I cannot pray to My Father, and He will provide Me with more than twelve legions of angels? How then could the Scriptures be fulfilled, that it must happen thus?" (Matthew 26:52–54 NKJV). Likewise, the Word of God will not be fulfilled in our lives if we live for our rights. God is more qualified than we are to defend and protect the rights he gives us.

Jesus was not concerned about his rights but about the fulfillment of the Scriptures. He left his rights in God's hands and carried out his God-given responsibilities. Likewise, we must follow our Lord. We should allow the Holy Spirit to fulfill the commandments of God in our lives. God called us to love, to be kind, to pray for our enemies, to serve, and so on. If we want to defend our rights, these Scriptures will not be fulfilled in our lives.

Wives, supporting our husbands for God's glory is one of our responsibilities. If our husbands sin, we ought to giving them our support by helping them get back to God because this is the right thing to do for our marriage (Galatians 6:1–3). If our husbands are living for God, we need to be their supporters by encouraging them in their service and serving God along with them.

We also need to be plugged into supportive groups composed of godly people who can help us become the kind of wives God wants us to be (Matthew 18:15–17). If we do what we can to support our husbands biblically, it is up to God to honor his Word in their lives. Our husbands sometimes may reject our support. This is beyond our control because God gives them freedom of choice as well, and he will hold them accountable for their choices. In the meantime, we can continue honoring God in what *we* choose.

Being a Support

It's helpful here to step back and look at God's overall design. God asks us to support our husbands, but this does not mean they should not support us as well. One-way support is ultimately destructive for our marriages. Hopefully, our husbands will give us the same level of support they expect from us. But this depends on their willingness to live for God. In God's design, marital support is a two-way road for husbands and wives to travel together. Jesus supports our husbands so that they can support us as their wives. "If the support is one way, though—if one carries most of the responsibility for providing emotional support for the other and gets little in return—that imbalance inevitably will create stress in the marriage. The supportive partner will get exhausted and very likely resentful, and the dependent partner will be disappointed when the level of support dips below what he or she has come to expect."[11]

God created marriage to be mutual and well-balanced, with both sides offering support. No one person can do everything at work or at home alone. God supports us so that we can support one another. We must work together to maintain a balanced life. The absence of loyal support in marriage will destroy marriage. God can help us develop and cultivate a spirit of helpfulness to one another and to uphold our husbands in fulfilling their God-given responsibilities.

So how do we support our husbands? In practical terms, what can we do in the real world to give them support and lift them up?

First, to support our husbands is to see the positive in them. We support our husbands when we are women of positivity who see the best in them. We did not marry our husbands because they were bad individuals. We fell in love with them because we saw good things in their lives that we liked. Those good qualities that drew us to our husbands are still in them. Perhaps we have allowed our unmet expectations or our husbands' shortcomings to cloud our minds to the good side of our love story. Dwelling on what our husbands do *not* do will not help our marriage.

As the first step to seeing the positive in our husbands, we need to develop a good mind through the teachings of Christ. We read in Philippians 4:8, "And now, dear brothers and sisters, one final thing. Fix your thoughts on what is true, and honorable, and right, and pure, and lovely, and admirable. Think about things that are excellent and worthy of praise." Writing down in our journals what good we see in our husbands is another powerful step in seeing the positive in their lives.

Second, to support our husbands is to praise them. After we choose to dwell on the positive, we need to practice the habit of praising our husbands with words of affirmation. This shows that we value them and appreciate what they are doing right. We need to use the heart of praise that God has given us through faith in Christ Jesus to speak well of our husbands. From the heart, our mouth will speak (Matthew 15:18). If we allow dirty thoughts to take root in our hearts, we will address our husbands with filthy language. If we allow criticism and judgment to fill our hearts, we will address our husbands with accusation and disapproval. If we fill our hearts with thoughts of their good qualities and actions, we will address our husbands with appreciation and praise.

Our praises to our husbands need to be sincere and clear. Describing specific things that our husbands do is important when we are praising them, because they need to know what we are commending them for. To praise our husbands is to be thankful to God.

Third, to support our husbands is to encourage them. To encourage our husbands is to build them up. We can build up our husbands in many ways. We can help them better their education, become more spiritual, and get more involved in ministry in the local church. We can build them up by giving them time to be with their friends. The list goes on and on when it comes to the things we can do to encourage our husbands.

Lifting the spirits of our husbands and giving them encouragement glorifies God and follows his desire for marriage. "So encourage each other and build each other up, just as you are already doing" (1 Thessalonians 5:11).

Of course, there are additional ways we can support our husbands, but we can begin with the three discussed here. If we can support other people, why can we not support our husbands? Think about it! What would happen if the employees of a company refused to support or submit to those who were in leadership roles? First, the company would not be able to deliver its products to the customers. Second, the employ-ees would be reprimanded or lose their jobs for rebelling against their authority. Employers hire employees to work according to the policy of the company. The moment they rebel, something must be done to solve the problem. Division is not a normal and acceptable practice. The rela-tionship between employers and employees must be smooth in order for a company to meet the needs of its clients.

The situation in a family is much the same. The moment Eve chose to rebel against God, she placed herself under the leadership of another authority, Satan. And the moment Adam rejected the leadership of God in order to submit himself to the leadership of his rebellious wife, Satan became their leader. Consequently, they experienced the punishment of their rebellion against God. Praise God, he intervened to bring order back into their marriage, and through their generations, into our world!

In Christ Jesus, we are now under the leadership of God. With God's Spirit, we can practice the discipline of submission and support. If we do not want to destroy our own marriages, we need to be the great support-ers that God wants us to be for our husbands. He knows our husbands need help. He made us to be the glory and support of our husbands. If we can submit our lives to other people to accomplish earthly goals, then it is even more important to submit to our own husbands for God's sake. We become wives when we support our husbands.

HELPING OUR HUSBANDS

"Then the Lord God said, 'It is not good for the man
to be alone. I will make a helper who is just right for him.'"
—GENESIS 2:18

enesis tells us that God created Adam first, in his own image. He equipped him with divine skills to be his representative on earth. God built a house for Adam before he made him. The house was called Paradise. He instructed Adam to manage the house for the well-being of himself, his family, and all mankind. God gave him abilities that were to be shown in the way he managed his house for the glory of the Creator.

God did something else, however. He realized that Adam could not perform the job of glorifying God and managing his house effectively alone. So God provided him a helper. He created for Adam a wonderful wife to make him whole. Adam called her Eve.

It is very important for the success of our marriages that we act as helpers to our husbands. Just as it was not good for Adam to be alone, it is not good for us to allow other duties of life to keep us from being with our husbands and assisting them in their God-given mission. Making our husbands feel our presence as the needed helpers God wants for them might help them see how valuable we are to complete them!

Like the topic of submission, "helping" can be very misunderstood. Some women may feel that helping their husbands is degrading. Nothing could be farther from the truth! My husband, Frantz, says this about my role as his helper:

"I am thankful to God for my wife. Without her, there is no way I would be able to be what I should be in the family. God knew that I needed a helper. And he gave me one. Thank you, my Father, for my wife! Life would be crazy without her in the house. Oftentimes I find myself inside of a Walmart, wandering around looking for stuff that my wife wants me to buy for cooking. If it were not for the helpers hired by those stores, I would have lost my way for good! I am grateful for the helpers who have rescued me many times. I am also thankful for the computer experts who have designed search engines to help me find what I need online. Oftentimes I do not know the meaning of words or am unable to locate web addresses, but Google, Bing, or Yahoo become my helper in finding what I need. Life without helpers is life without knowing. And not knowing what to do makes life difficult. My wife is my helper, keeping me from losing my way and helping me know what to do in life. I don't know what life would be like without her!"

Since we do not know all things, we all need helpers. Since we cannot do all things alone, we all need other people to help us out. God wired men and women with differences. And those differences make us mutually dependent on each other. For example, most men can only focus on one thing at a time, while most women can focus on many things at a time. This is a requirement for mothering. A woman can be on the phone, cooking, helping the kids with homework, and doing other things all at the same time. If a man has to play the mother role in the family for even a few minutes, he becomes confused, not knowing what to do, because God did not wire him to be a multitasker!

Women and men both came from the same source. God made them both in his image. Yet he made them *male and female*. We are different by divine design so that we can complement each other.

Women, we are the helpers of our husbands. A helper is someone who gives to another person what he needs to function as he should. In Hebrew, the word translated "helper" also means to share a task with someone, to rescue, to bring a reinforcement, to take in hand, or to establish firmly.

Because we understand the plan of God and want to glorify him, we choose not to capitalize on our husbands' failures, weaknesses, and imperfections. We choose not to criticize them. We prefer to rescue, comfort, and help them be the husbands and the men God intended them to be. *God created us to complete our husbands, not to compete with them.* He wants our words and actions to contribute to the well-being of our husbands. Our husbands cannot be all that they ought to be in the family without our help. The Lord God said, "It is not good that man should be alone; I will make him a helper comparable to him" (Genesis 2:18 NKJV). God did not create us to work against our husbands, but for them (1 Corinthians 11:9). We mutually depend on one another to establish a godly marriage. God knew that it was not good for our husbands to be alone. They need us to assist them in accomplishing his plans.

In thinking about our role as helpers, we need to focus on different ways to help our husbands. These ways are biblical principles to a successful marriage.

Giving Spiritual Help to Our Husbands

According to Jesus in John 6:63, spirituality is obtained and sustained through the Spirit, who gives a combination of life and the words of God that are life and spirit. Once we become spiritual wives through a Spirit-led life and a life saturated with the words of Jesus, we will be able to provide spiritual assistance to our husbands.

Spirituality is not brought about by human effort but by divine gift. God made us to be spiritual helpers to our husbands. Yet like Eve, who failed to help her husband spiritually and instead obeyed Satan, we may fail to give spiritual help to our husbands if we listen to Satan rather than obeying God. Often, Satan's voice comes through the expectations and depictions of our culture. Our culture promotes competition within marriages instead of obedience to God's plan for marriage, where we are asked to complete one another. Completion is God's will for marriage, whereas competition between spouses is Satan's goal to destroy a godly marriage. With the help of men and women who submit their wills to the devil, many marriages become places of selfishness where everyone says and does what is good for themselves.

With that battle always raging around us, spiritual help is designed by God to promote and strengthen marriage. We can be a source of spiritual encouragement to our husbands in at least three ways.

First, we need to pray for our husbands and with our husbands. God is carefully listening to our prayers because he wants to establish a loving bond between us and our husbands. In order to pray effectively, we must know and obey the teachings of Christ, because God will answer prayers that are in alignment with what Jesus reveals to us about his Father. Focusing on God's promises as revealed in the Bible will help us pray according to his will, thus guaranteeing a satisfactory answer. "Now this is the confidence that we have in Him, that if we ask anything, according to His will, He hears us" (1 John 5:14 NKJV). We need to humbly commune with God on behalf of our husbands so that he can help them be his men in the family.

When things are not going well in the marriage relationship, nagging or criticizing our husbands or gossiping about them with our friends or relatives will be detrimental to the intimacy and success of our marriage. Considerable quarrels are likely to occur when we do not bring our marital needs to God in prayer—the One who is able to change lives. Great and amazing things happen in our lives, families, and environments when we humble ourselves before God, desiring to please him in everything. Hannah did just that (1 Samuel 1:9-19). Esther poured out her heart to God in prayer and fasting for her people (Esther 4:15-16). Praying for our husbands is a biblical way of telling God how much we love them.

Second, we can give spiritual help when we fast for our husbands. According to *Vine's Expository Dictionary,* fasting is "a voluntary abstinence from food." Sometimes there are things in our lives, as well as in the lives of our husbands, that can only be dealt with by giving up food and other important activities in order to concentrate on prayer and seek God for our families. Queen Esther prayed, fasted, and waited for God's timing before she talked to her husband, the king, about something important. When Mordecai inquired about Esther's disposition to help save his people, her reply to him was, "Go, gather all the Jews who are present in Shushan, and fast for me; neither eat nor drink for three days, night or day. My maids and I will fast likewise. And so I will go to the king, which is against the law; and if I perish, I perish!" (Esther 4:16).

If your husband does things to you that are against God's law, you can always seek God's help for him through fasting. One important note here: We are not suggesting anyone stay in an abusive relationship in the name of religion. Jesus came to heal the brokenhearted and to set the captives free (Luke 4:18). God did not make marriage for husbands to make their wives suffer but to love them. No woman would have married a man if he had promised during the wedding ceremony that he would abuse her. When a man stops being the loving husband God wants him to be, the right thing to do is to seek help from God and godly counselors to bring their marriage back to glorifying God. In an abusive situation, wives will better serve their husbands by getting some distance until a godly solution is found for their problems. Asking God to help you be a good wife does not mean letting your husband abuse you either verbally or physically. Seek help and pray. No matter how long you have to pray and fast for your husband to become what God wants him to be, the time will not be wasted.

Women who face less extreme situations may still suffer in their relationships. It is here that fasting and prayer becomes especially appropriate. Even though you are married, sometimes you may feel like you are a widow because your husband is not there for you when you need him due to his careless attitude. There is a woman mentioned in the Bible, a widow named Anna, whose example we can follow. "This woman was a widow of about eighty-four years, who did not depart from the temple, but served God with fasting and prayers night and day" (Luke 2:37 NKJV). How did she serve God? She did it through fasting and prayers. We can do the same for our husbands and our families. Through fasting, we allow the Holy Spirit to strengthen us to face whatever problems God may allow to come in our lives.

Third, we can help our husbands by encouraging them to obey the Word of God. God can use us to influence our husbands to study his Word and obey him. If our husbands see that we study the Bible daily and notice the changes that God's Word produces in our lives, they will inquire about what is going on with us. Then we can seek a commitment from our husbands to study the Bible with us. (A couple's devotional Bible may be helpful to start with.) We read in the Bible of a couple who obeyed the Lord together: "There was in the days of Herod, the king of Judea, a certain priest named Zacharias . . . His wife was one of the daughters of Aaron; her name was Elizabeth. And they were both righteous before God, walking in all the commandments and ordinances of the Lord blameless" (Luke 1:5–6 NKJV). What a great example for a couple to follow!

God asks all his children to encourage one another in the faith: "Therefore comfort each other and edify one another, just as you also are doing" (1 Thessalonians 5:11 NKJV). As helpers, we need to ask questions about our husbands' regularity in church, the exercise of their ministries, their perseverance in meditating on God's Word, and gently encourage them in these areas. This might be a long process that requires us to be patient with our husbands. But through our consistent prayers, the Lord can make our husbands into men of the Bible, men who constantly live in compliance with the commandments of God and are thus enabled to stand firm in the Lord. Their relationship with God will help them know what is right and will also equip them with godly skills to live with us as godly husbands.

When We Hurt Our Husbands Spiritually

When someone designed to give help gives hurt instead, the results can be extremely destructive. The Bible is full of examples of wives who were not a spiritual help to their husbands. The first such wife mentioned is Eve. "So when the woman saw that the tree was good for food, that it was pleasant to the eyes, and a tree desirable to make one wise, she took of its fruit and ate. She also gave to her husband with her, and he ate" (Genesis 3:6 NKJV). Eve failed to help her husband live in spiritual communion with God; she guided and influenced him into sin and ruin.

Jezebel is another example. In the affair of Naboth and the vineyard, she encouraged her husband, Ahab, to sin. "Then Jezebel his wife said to him, 'You now exercise authority over Israel! Arise, eat food, and let your heart be cheerful; I will give you the vineyard of Naboth the Jezreelite.' But there was no one like Ahab who sold himself to do wickedness in the sight of the Lord, because Jezebel his wife stirred him up" (1 King 21:7, 25 NKJV).

We need to carefully consider what kind of advice we are giving our husbands. Remember, they are designed to need our help—so our advice carries more weight than we realize! Since God knows everything, we would be wise to seek his wisdom through the pages of the Bible and the guidance of his Spirit before we advise our husbands. It is not good for our relationship with God to stir up our husbands to do what is wicked in the eyes of the Lord.

When Job faced a time of extreme suffering and loss, his wife encouraged her husband to curse God and die. "Then his wife said to him, 'Do you still hold fast to your integrity? Curse God and die!' But he said to her, 'You speak as one of the foolish women speaks. Shall we indeed accept good from God, and shall we not accept adversity?' In all of this, Job did not sin with his lips" (Job 2:9–10 NKJV).

We need to pray so we do not counsel our husbands to break God's Word. We also need to watch our own lives so that we don't give them a reason to listen to the counsel of wicked people (Psalm 1:1). For example, we sometimes ask our husbands to borrow money to buy us stuff we know they cannot afford. That will eventually keep them at work away from us because they need pay back our debt. Proverbs 14:1 says that a wise woman builds her house, but a foolish woman tears it down with her own hands. Let's be wise women, encouraging our husbands and building our homes through the way we speak and live!

There is a time to speak and a time to pray, and blessed is the man whose wife can discern between the two. "Better to dwell in the wilderness than with a contentious and angry woman" (Proverbs 21:19 NKJV). "To everything there is a season, a time for every purpose under heaven: A time to tear, and a time to sew; a time to keep silence, and a time to speak" (Ecclesiastes 3:1, 7 NKJV). Ask the Lord to show you when to speak and when to be quiet. We can follow the example of spiritual women in the Bible to be what God wants for our marriage and our generation.

Providing Material Help to Our Husbands

We can help our husbands with material help as well. In our modern age, this is a need for more and more couples. Priscilla and her husband Aquila had the same profession, and they worked for and with each other (Acts 18:1–3). Paul praised and thanked Priscilla, the wife of Aquila, for her generosity to him and to God's work through her tent-making business (Romans 16:3–4). She used her business to provide material help to her husband.

Priscilla and Aquila were business partners without letting their work have negative effects on their marital relationship. They worked together to promote their marriage and to enhance the kingdom of God. Furthermore, the wife mentioned in Proverbs 31 got praise from her husband and children partly for her industrious and managerial abilities. She bought items and worked from her home to support her husband and family materially.

So yes, we can give material help to our husbands in the area of finances. *However, it's important to understand that it is not a moral obligation or a divine order for the wife to contribute 50 percent toward the expenses of the home, as some people in today's society want to impose.* It is mainly the responsibility of the husband to work for his wife and family. If a wife can and wants to, she can help with the expenses of the family, but the husband should not make it an obligation on her. A wife's priority should be her husband, not a job.

Once a wife becomes a mother, she now has another responsibility—the full-time job of motherhood. With the duties of wife and motherhood already on her, a husband under normal circumstances should not expect his wife to have another full-time job and on top of that work in the house. This is too overwhelming for any woman!

Frantz says that these days, he guesses some husbands become lazy because they want their wives to work for them. He also says this is a disgrace and an occasion to blaspheme the Word of God! I agree. God gave Adam work in the garden *before* he presented Eve to him to be his wife. "The Lord God placed the man in the Garden of Eden to tend and watch over it." Then the Lord God said, "It is not good for the man to be alone. I will make a helper who is just right for him" (Genesis 2:15, 18). Eve, the helper of Adam, came into his life after God had already given Adam the opportunity to work so he could provide for his wife. If a husband can and wants to work, God has a job for him on earth to do in order to feed his wife whom he loves.

One spouse cannot do everything in the home. Managing a home requires teamwork between a husband and a wife. The principle of delegation must be applied so that responsibilities are shared. Many wives are like Moses when he was trying to judge all of the people of Israel by himself. Wives who are trying to do too much in the house need to listen to the Word of God and delegate some of the household duties to their husbands, who cannot refuse because they love their wives. (If your husband does refuse to help you, God knows all about it and will reward your service and your prayers. Keep seeking him for your husband to become the husband he needs to be.)

Moses's father-in-law, Jethro, saw that Moses was overburdened by the task he had taken on. Jethro advised him to divide the duties of judgment so that Moses would be able to endure the pressures of his position (Exodus 18:14–24). A burden-free marriage is one where the couple listens to God's command to use the principle of delegation because of mutual love for one another. It is too heavy of a burden for the wife to handle everything in the house by herself.

So if we don't want to take over our husbands' positions or give all our energy to a job outside the home, how we can assist our husbands financially? We can do so in at least three ways.

First, if we and our husbands are in mutual agreement, we can work outside the home (Ruth 2:6–7, 23). However, we need to remember that our primary responsibility is toward God and toward our husbands and to our family and home. We need to be good wives to our husbands first, and second we need to be good mothers, rather than having a career that might keep us away from our marriage and family. Careers can be important, but they should not come at the expense of our marriages.

Of course, as we have already touched on, working outside the home becomes more complicated when we become mothers. This is a crucial time to pray and communicate with our husbands about our work and home responsibilities, because children cannot raise themselves. They need their parents. Our children are far more important and valuable than having a few more dollars in the bank to buy things that have no eternal value, and staying home with our children can be more rewarding than any career outside the home. When a mother is thinking about working outside the home, she needs to decide what is best for her relationship with God, her husband, and her children.

Second, we can work in our own enterprises at home to help our husbands. The Bible offers several examples of women who did this: Dorcas, the charitable seamstress (Acts 9:36–39); Lydia, the cloth merchant (Acts 16:14–15); and the virtuous woman of Proverbs 31, just to name a few. These women were working at their own enterprises not only to help their families, but also to enhance the kingdom of God. God can help us find creative ways to use our God-given abilities to open our own businesses so that we can help our husbands financially and invest in the kingdom of God as well!

Third, we can help our husbands financially by wisely managing the income of the family and avoiding needless purchases. This will help us live within the means of the family. Finally, we can also help our husbands by making sure that food and other resources are not wasted. After Jesus fed the five thousand, he told his disciples, "Gather up the fragments that remain, so that nothing is lost" (John 6:12 NKJV). We need to give thanks to the Lord for our meals and other provisions rather than throwing his blessings in the trashcan.

Satisfying the Sexual Needs of Our Husbands

We help our husbands when we satisfy their sexual needs. It is God's will for marriage that we share our beauty and our sexuality with our husbands. After God blessed Adam and his wife, he told them to make love so that they could multiply and fill the earth with his image (Genesis 1:28). God blesses us to meet the sexual needs of our husbands as well. We are beautiful for our own husbands, and we keep ourselves sexy for our husbands only. The same principle applies to our husbands as well. The Bible says: "Nevertheless, because of sexual immorality, let each man have his own wife, and let each woman have her own husband. Let the husband render to his wife the affection due to her, and likewise the wife to her husband. The wife does not have authority over her body, but the husband does. Likewise, the husband does not have authority over his body, but the wife does. Do not deprive one another except with consent for a time that you may give yourselves to fasting and prayer; and come together again so that Satan does not tempt you because of your lack of self-control" (1 Corinthian 7:2–5 NKJV).

Having good sex with our husbands is God's wonderful idea for our marriage. In marriage, we share our bodies willingly and freely with each other without holding back. With God's help, we can relate more effectively and more tenderly to each other's sexual needs. Proverbs 5:15–20 depicts this relationship beautifully:

"Drink from your own cistern, and running water from your own well. Should your fountain be dispersed abroad, streams of water in the streets? Let them be only your own, and not for strangers with you. Let your fountain be blessed and rejoice with the wife of your youth. As a loving doe, let her breasts satisfy you at all times; and always be enraptured with her love"(NKJV).

When Things Are Out of Order

Back in Genesis, we saw that the divine order was that Adam was to be in charge of the house and Eve was to help him. Not the other way around. A conflict can emerge in our marriages when husbands reverse the "divine order" and think we come into their lives to free them from the normal service they used to do before marriage. Some might say, "I am married now, so I do not have to do anything in the house. My wife will take care of everything. My job is to work outside the home to provide for the family."

Being the main provider for the family is part of the truth for husbands, but it's only *part* of it. Adam was not only responsible to work, he was also responsible to keep the garden in order. Husbands who think housework is only for their wives really believe they are helpers and their wives are the main person running the show! If this issue remains unaddressed, it will likely sabotage the divine dynamics of our marriage. As wives, we will become overwhelmed with the responsibilities of the family while our husbands have too much leeway to be idle.

How should we react if this is the behavior of our husbands? Although it is generally hard for us not to complain about it, complaining will not resolve the problem. We need to respectfully find ways to assist our husbands to understand that God made us to be their helpers, not their replacements. It is important that we reflect on this concern and bring it to the attention of our husbands. One thing we can do is learn communication and conflict resolution skills to help our husbands more effectively.

A good way to start the conversation might be to use an illustration. We might say something like this: "Honey, suppose that you are lifting something heavy at work, and you ask someone to help you out because the load is too heavy. Would it be right to leave and let the helper do the lifting alone?"

Pause and give your husband time to answer. A reasonable husband will probably say, "Of course not! It would be irresponsible on my part to ask for help and then turn my back on the one who comes to help me. That would not be the right thing to do at all."

Then you can calmly and lovingly respond to your husband with something like this. "Sweetheart, I know you love me because you work hard to provide for my needs, for which I am grateful. God gave me to you to be your helper in our marriage, and I am happy to help out with the duties of the house. But sometimes I feel like I am doing everything by myself. I come to help you, but it seems that you let me carry the load alone. God knew there are many things you cannot do as well as I can, so in his love and kindness he gave me to you to assist you. But it seems like you withdraw yourself completely from the household duties to be occupied only with activities outside the home. Even if you are at home, you prefer to do what you like while I am killing myself with everything else in the house. God gave Adam the garden, which was his house to occupy, perhaps so that he could realize how difficult it was to work alone. Then God saw that it was not good for him to be alone, and he met his needs by giving him Eve. My love, before you married me, you used to do everything alone, but God put me in your life to help you so you would not have to do that anymore. Since you are my leader, I want to express my concerns to you so you can resolve the problem. Thank you for listening to me, my love."

If your husband responds affirmatively to your request, you can suggest that you both go out to eat at his favorite restaurant to talk more about your relationship and to identify and articulate ways you can increase marriage intimacy and partnership.

Seeking help from Christian counselors should be considered if your husband remains uncooperative. Yet most importantly, you must talk with your heavenly Father about the situation. Pray something like this: "My Father in heaven, I feel abandoned by my husband, just like my Lord Jesus felt abandoned by you on Calvary. I've talked with my husband about how I feel, but he is unresponsive. I need your help, my Daddy. You will never leave me nor forsake me, and you love me unconditionally. Be my refuge and strength, and help my husband to see me as his helper. Perhaps he will appreciate me as his helper and glorify you. Please continue to help me be the wife you want me to be for my husband."

Helping and the Holy Spirit

As godly wives, God has called us to the role of helpers of our husbands, knowing that we will one day give account to him. The Holy Spirit is the Helper of all the children of God. What the Holy Spirit is to us as our Helper is what we are to our husbands as their helpers. We are the ones our husbands waited for in order to be complete, just like the disciples waited for the Holy Spirit before they could become effective witnesses for Jesus Christ. The Holy Spirit empowered them to fulfill the will of God. In the same way, God made us to empower our husbands to do his will. That is why God said it was not good for man to be alone. We are good news to our husbands because God made us to help them. They are no longer alone because we make them whole.

Father, please gives us the help that we need to fulfill this role, rejoicing in it, and surrendering to it because we want to glorify you. Thank you for being our Helper to help our husbands!

GIVING GRACE
TO OUR HUSBANDS

"A gracious woman gains respect,
but ruthless men gain only wealth."
—PROVERBS 11:16

I t is amazing to see how perfectly God plans everything out in marriage so that each person can be used as an instrument to reveal some of God's invisible attributes to the other. For instance, he uses the husband as the means for the wife to experience God's love in marriage. Thus, he commands the husband to love his wife. On the other hand, the husband experiences God's grace through the wife. Our husbands give us love, while we give them grace.

Women become wives when we are gracious to our husbands. Through the indwelling presence of the Spirit of God in our hearts, we live with our husbands with grace. We are full of grace so that we can be godly helpers to them for the glory of our God. Look again at the verse that opens this chapter. Since we are gracious wives, we preserve the esteem and respect of our husbands in the same way strong men keep possession of their wealth. Our husbands praise us both in private and public because they experience God's grace through us (Proverbs 31:28). The members of the family, the people in the church, and the citizens of the community honor and esteem our husbands because we are gracious wives. A good reputation is preferable to riches (Proverbs 22:1a). We give that to our husbands in the way we live with them.

Giving the Grace of Our Lips

There are several ways we can give grace to our husbands. First, we give it with our lips—in other words, we give it through the way we speak and the things we say. One of the meanings of *grace* is to appeal and to charm. This type of grace is revealed in the way we use our tongues when talking to our husbands. Proverbs 5:19 tells us, "*As a* loving deer and a graceful doe, Let her breasts satisfy you at all times; And always be enraptured with her love." The woman in this passage is referred to as "a graceful doe." A few chapters later, we read, "The words of the godly are a life-giving fountain; the words of the wicked conceal violent intentions. Whoever loves a pure heart and gracious speech will have the king as a friend" (Proverbs 10:11, 22:11). By contrast, "Wise people treasure knowledge, but the babbling of a fool invites disaster" (Proverbs 10:14). The woman of wisdom graciously tells the truth to her husband because she loves him. She knows that "lying lips are an abomination unto the LORD" (Proverbs 12:22 NKJV). What a blessing for our husbands to dwell with graceful and gracious wives like us! We also let God use our spiritual and physical beauty to charm our husbands (and them only!).

With words that come from our hearts, we graciously speak the truth in love to our husbands. Because we are good wives by God's grace, we live out the truth with a clear conscience in words and actions as we relate to our husbands. Gracious words are respectful and honorable. The truth must never bow down before lies, but it must always be professed in love (Ephesians 4:15). Grace in our hearts for our husbands will not allow us to communicate with them with foolish words.

Because we are gracious wives, we respect and honor our husbands in how we articulate our concerns. Although some of us may be more talkative than our husbands, we can let God's Spirit help us control our tongues so we can discern when to talk or not to talk. We read in Proverbs 10:18–19: "Whoever hides hatred has lying lips, and whoever spreads slander is a fool. In the multitude of words sin is not lacking, but he who restrains his lips is wise." When Satan tempts us to use our lips to destroy our husbands with words spoken, we decline and speak instead with wisdom, using words that are sweeter than honey.

Emotionally, we can either kill or save our husbands with our lips. With our mouths, we can destroy our husbands instead of being gracious wives to them (Proverbs 11:9). Some wives feel free to secretly slander their husbands to friends and family members. This will destroy the loving bond, which exists between our husbands and us. In marriage, we become one with our husbands. If we criticize our husbands, it is like criticizing ourselves. God condemns this nonsense attitude. "Whoever secretly slanders his neighbor, him I will destroy" (Psalm 101:5a NKJV). Our husbands' shortcomings are not designed for us to gossip around with our friends, coworkers, and family members. Instead, we need to use our lips with the influence of God's Spirit to communicate with our husbands in a manner that is worthy of our calling as children of God. We were not created to raise our voices when talking to our husbands, but to express our thoughts tenderly so we can bring out the best in them. Our mouths are instrumental in creating intimacy and encouraging our husbands to serve our Lord.

We can also give grace to our husbands by kissing our husbands with our loving lips. We should kiss with passion on a regular basis to stimulate intimacy. Invite your husband to come and see how soft and loving are your lips, with a big smile in your face. We kiss our husbands the same way we want to be kissed, and we graciously make them happy with the sweetness of our lips.

Giving the Grace of Our Actions

The word *grace* also means kindness and undeserved favor. We can show these things through our actions, not just our words. Because we are considerate wives whose grace is modeled after the grace of Christ, we do not do anything for our husbands because they deserve it. *Rather, our husbands are blessed because they find grace in what we do for them.* We show kindness and sweetness toward our husbands when we prepare their meals and serve them. We use our soft and loving hands to express our love to our husbands through passionate physical touch. We look out for their needs and meet them with kindness. The Bible teaches us that grace is better than money and gold (Proverbs 22:1b). We are better to our husbands than wealth because we are gracious wives.

We model God's grace to our husbands in how we treat them even when they sin against us. We give them forgiveness for sin, goodness for evil deeds, and love for hatred because we want them to see God's grace through us. We let God use us as a vehicle through which he can reveal his grace toward our husbands in every way. If we fall short of living graciously with our husbands, we ask for forgiveness.

Giving the Grace of a Crown

We give grace to our husbands when we become their crown of glory. As their crown, we represent honor, success, and victory for our husbands. We crown our husbands in how we feed them, dress them (chicly and nicely), equip them to carry themselves in public, and give them a peaceful home where they may rest in our loving arms. Being their crown has a lot to do with the reputation we give our husbands in our home and community, how we are good to them, and how we give them happiness. We do not cause shame to our husbands, because we are gracious wives.

We read in Proverbs 12:4 these words: "An excellent wife is the crown of her husband, but the wife who causes shame is like rottenness in his bone"(NKJV). It is important to note from this verse that we are to not be a painful crown of thorns to our husbands, but rather a crown of glory. To be a painful crown is to bring problems to our husbands. We know very well that if we become a crown of thorns to them, our husbands' minds will be crowded with painful thoughts, and they will not be able to think effectively—which will have direct ramifications in our relationship with them. If our husbands, who are the leaders of our homes, cannot properly form their thoughts, then the members of the family will have to bear the misery—especially us!

Instead, because we are gracious wives, we look to God to find good ways to help our husbands so they can think biblically. We understand our duties in marriage, and we are vessels of honor through whom God can comfort our husbands. God made us to be the glory of our husbands.

Giving the Grace of Wisdom

We give grace to our husbands when we live wisely with them. Our marriage will be built or demolished by our wisdom or our foolishness. With God's wisdom, we build our relationship with our husbands and construct our home with eternal gifts such as love, mercy, grace, holiness, and peace. In dealing with our husbands with wisdom, we will multiply the days of our marriage and add years to our lives. We read in Proverbs 14:1 these wonderful words: "The wise woman builds her house, but the foolish pulls it down with her hands"(NKJV). We are also the force and sustainer of our homes (Proverbs 9:1).

Wisdom is the application of God's Word. God provides us with resources in the Scripture and in the Holy Spirit to build our homes. There cannot be any real wisdom except in an intimate relationship with God through Jesus. Jesus is our wisdom (1 Corinthians 1:30). We experience his wisdom as we obey his teaching in our relationship with our husbands. Although the ingenuity and wealth of human beings are important, we cannot build a home where love and peace reign without the help of God (Proverbs 10:22 and Galatians 5:22). God is the source of wisdom. Our fear of God causes us to be wise. As we lovingly fear him and learn his ways, we will let him be the builder, the protector, and the provider of our marriage (Psalm 127).

Giving the Grace of Love

Finally, we give grace to our husbands when we learn to love them. Grace enables us as wives to love our husbands, and with the help of other godly women, we learn to love them and our children. "These older women must train the younger women to love their husbands and their children" (Titus 2:4). If you are not yet married, you must guard yourself from the company of foolish women if you want to learn how to love your husband and build your home on wisdom in order to enjoy happy days in your marriage. If you have already married, we advise you to let God guide you to some godly women who can teach you how to love your husband and your children.

Loving a husband is neither automatic nor easy. For us as wives, love is not our primary function in marriage—instead, we are called to lovingly respect our husbands. Nevertheless, God intends for love to grow out of this relationship. Where can we go to learn how to love our husbands when challenges arise?

First, we can learn how to love our husbands from mature spiritual women in the Christian family. As we have already read, the older women must be teachers of love to the young wives. However, not every aged woman is eligible to teach other women how to love their husbands. We cannot teach others to love if we have never known and lived out love ourselves. God's love must be in the heart of aged women before they can teach young women how to love their husbands. They must be qualified biblically. The required qualifications are their faith in God, godly conduct, and life experience. Their conduct must be holy and good in order for them to teach their wives how to love their husbands. Those aged women become teachers of love to other women because they love and honor God in demonstrating holy and good conduct toward their own husbands. Pray to God that he would give you a mentor who can teach you how to better love your husband.

Second, we can learn how to love our husbands from our husbands themselves. Frantz would say "Amen" to this! Our husbands can articulate to us better than anyone else how we can love them. Perhaps we might ask them a question like this: "What is your greatest need, my sweetheart?" The answer to this question can be a good indicator in knowing how to love your husband. Once we know what our husbands consider to be their greatest need, we will understand how to meet that need with our love. May I suggest to you that sexual intercourse might be his answer? If that is true, then love him with all the spiritual and physical beauties that God has given you. Make yourself beautiful and sexy for your husband.

Whatever your husband's answer might be, ask God to help you love him. Loving your husband means satisfying his needs.

Lastly, we can learn how to love our husbands from God himself. Who made the husband? The answer is God (Genesis 1:27). Who knows the husband? The answer is God (Psalm 139:1–18). Who is the source of love? The answer is God (1 John 4:8). Who gives the ability to love unconditionally? The answer is God (John 14:26, Galatians 5:22). Who first loved us? The answer is God (1 John 4:18). So the best Person to teach us how to truly love our husbands is God himself.

We must experience God's love in order to love the husbands he gave to us. Our love for our husbands is contingent on the love of God for us. God gave us his best: Jesus Christ (Romans 5:8). God so loves us that he gave Jesus to die in our place (John 3:16). If being loved by God means receiving the best of God in Jesus, then we will love our husbands when we give our best to them. God poured his love into the hearts of his children so that we might love like him. Love makes us hopeful about our husbands, and as Romans 5:5 reminds us, this hope will not lead to disappointment.

Giving Our Best

We give our husbands our best in everything to show them love: our best service, our best time, our best touch, our best words, our best conduct, and more. We need to make our husbands feel our love by talking the love and walking the love in our relationship with them. "We know what real love is because Jesus gave up His life for us. So we also ought to give up our lives for our brothers and sisters. If someone has enough money to live well and sees a brother or sister in need but shows no compassion—how can God's love be in that person? Dear children, let's not merely say that we love each other; let us show the truth by our actions" (1 John 3:16–18).

In all of these ways, we become wives when we live graciously with our husbands.

GIVING RESPECT TO OUR HUSBANDS

"So again I say, each man must love his wife as he loves himself, and the wife must respect her husband."
—EPHESIANS 5:33

R espect is a big deal for our husbands. In fact, from our husband's point of view, I will go so far as to say that *everything we do for them is meaningless if we do not respect them.* Our husbands want to lay the foundation of their marriage on our respect for them as their wives.

Dr. Kevin Leman said, "Without respect, there is nothing to build your marriage on. There's no foundation. If you can't respect your husband, you might as well call it quits, because your marriage isn't going to make it. Here's the even bigger issue behind respect. A man needs to feel your respect in order to love you the way you want to be loved. If he doesn't feel your respect, he won't climb out of his turtle shell to risk loving you because he might get hurt."

Men desperately need our respect to function well as our husbands. A man's number-one need from his wife is her respect. When a husband chooses to love his wife and a wife decides to respect her husband, their marriage will glorify God and their children will live happily. The husband and the wife will thank God for the marriage. On the other hand, the absence of love and respect in marriage brings many misfortunes to a couple.

Some wives disrespect their husbands because their personal needs are not being met. But displaying disrespectful conduct toward our husbands will not make our marriage better! Seeking our husband's forgiveness and asking God for forgiveness can heal the relationship. The Bible says: "Confess your sins to each other and pray for each other so that you may be healed. The earnest prayer of a righteous person has great power and produces wonderful results" (James 5:16). Please forgive us, Lord, for we know not what we are doing!

Even when our husbands are acting like ungodly men, we ought to make every effort to respect them just because God asks us to be respectful. We should not allow our emotions to lead to disrespectful talk and actions toward our husbands. God has called us to be filled with his Spirit to live out what he commands us to do. He demands that we respect our husbands for his glory. When the Holy Spirit leads us, we will respect our husbands in our thoughts, our words, and our actions.

Our physical expressions when we are chatting with our husbands can show whether we respect them. Displaying an ungodly attitude toward our husbands is a sign of disrespect. Yelling at our husbands does not show them that we respect them. Would we act the same way if we were talking to the president of our country? Of course not! Even if we disagreed with his policies, we would still treat him with respect. Then why do we think it is permissible to do that to the men we have chosen to become our husbands?

God has placed our husbands in a position of leadership in our marriages. We ought to give the utmost respect that is due to them as our heads. If they are kings of the house, we are their queens. Therefore, we should give them the royal treatment daily and watch to see the positive impact it will have on us and the entire family. Begin today to deal with your husband like a king, and do it with a loving heart and godly attitude.

What is a husband's greatest need? You may be thinking money, education, power, sex, or fame. All these things are important; however, they cannot fulfill a man's biggest need within the family. If you interviewed many couples and asked married women to tell you their greatest need, they would say it is for love. Wives cry out for their husbands' love day and night. When a wife is not satisfied with her relationship with her husband, she usually says, "My husband does not love me." Why does a wife cry for love? The answer is simple: God has created the man to become a husband so he can love his wife as Christ loves the church.

Meanwhile, if you ask a husband what he needs the most from his wife, he will tell you "respect." The husband *needs* to be respected by his wife. The wife cries for love, whereas the husband longs for respect. The reason for this is that God established him as the head of the family. As such, he must be respected.

According to the Bible, a wife's attitude must be characterized by deep respect for her husband. "Nevertheless, let each one of you in particular so love his own wife as himself, and let the wife see that she respects her husband" (Ephesians 5:33 NKJV).

The wife is to respect her husband because of his position. God has ordained your husband to be the head of the family, and as such he deserves to be respected. Some men are not godly husbands, and that is a disgrace to both God and the family. But when the husband is not what God intended him to be, we do not have to change the roles God established for marriage! We can bring the situation to the One who is the head of the man, Jesus Christ. He alone can change our husbands. If we choose to have an ungodly attitude toward our husbands when they do not love us, we will bring more misery to their souls, and the matter will still not be resolved. In fact, our attitude will help advance the plan of the devil, whose ultimate goal is to destroy our marriages.

Suppose you enter into a room with many people present whom you do not know. Perhaps you greet them and share a few words in order to get acquainted. What if you discover that one of the people in the room is the president of your country? I can guarantee that your attitude will automatically change toward him simply because of his office! You may not like everything he does, but you will give him the respect that is due to his position. Likewise, you may not agree with the character or the conduct of your husband; nevertheless, you should respect him because of his office and your love for God. If your husband does not love you, it is because he is spiritually blind. At that point, you must present your case to the Lord and continue to represent his grace in your marriage. Jesus can open the eyes of the blind. He can turn darkness into light right before your husband's eyes so that he can see the path of holiness.

We are precious in God's sight, and he loves us with an everlasting love. He promises to always be with us even through valleys of death. This is true in our marriages just as anywhere else. "When you pass through the waters, I will be with you; and through the rivers, they shall not overflow you. When you walk through the fire, you shall not be burned, nor shall the flame scorch you. For I am the LORD your God, the Holy One of Israel, your Savior" (Isaiah 43:2–3 NKJV). We can trust him with our husbands!

Practical Ways to Respect Our Husbands

There are five basic ways we can respect our husbands. *First, to respect our husbands is to honor them.* Since we are Christian wives who belong to Jesus Christ, we must hold our husbands in high esteem. Sarah honored her husband in spite of his failures. She called him "Lord" (1 Peter 3:3–6). Abraham could not give her what she desired the most—a child. Nevertheless, she honored him, and the Lord blessed her for her obedience.

Sarah adorned herself with an inner spiritual beauty. One of the aspects of this beauty consisted of a respectful submissiveness to her husband. We submit to our husbands and honor them not out of fear and servility, but because we want to do what is pleasing to God.

Second, to respect our husbands is to admire them. To *admire* means to give high regard. That implies approving and appreciating something or someone. When we admire our husbands, we will say the opposite of the mean things we have been saying to dismantle their manhood. If we do not show and verbalize admiration for our husbands, neither will we respect them as we should.

Our admiration for our husbands leads to consideration as well. The act of considering our husbands means to give them special attention.

It is impossible to respect one whom you do not consider. When we picture our husband in our mind as an important person in the family, one worthy of our admiration and regard, we will demonstrate that by our respectful attitude toward him. However, if we view our husband as just one more man on the street, then we will treat him as such. The way we think about our husbands in our minds is the way we relate to them. If we think highly of our husbands because God gave them to us, we will show them respect, which will lead to marriage intimacy.

Third, to respect our husbands is to be kind to them. We demonstrate our respect toward our husbands by speaking to them with kindness. Our kind words will heal the illnesses that weaken the souls of our husbands. We notice in Proverbs 16:24 the value of kind words: "Pleasant words are like a honeycomb, sweetness to the soul and health to the bones"(NKJV). When we constantly yell at and belittle our husbands, this is our way of telling them, "I do not respect or value you; you are nothing." Some wives give more respect to their supervisor at work than they do to their husband. They treat other men more kindly than their own husbands. Isn't that sad? When we disrespect our husbands, we disrespect Christ, because he is the head of every man.

The consequences of disrespecting our husband can be catastrophic. Michal, King David's wife, paid a huge price for her lack of respect for her husband. God's judgment caused her to be unable to ever bear children (2 Samuel 6:16–23). In another biblical example, Queen Vashti refused to obey her husband's command. As a result, she lost her position as queen (Esther 1).

If you have been living with your husband in a disrespectful way, we encourage you to talk to God about it. He holds you accountable for what you do. Ask him to forgive you. When you've done that, you also need to sit down with your husband to talk things over. Point out to your husband areas in which you have not been the type of wife God wants you to be to him. Ask him to forgive you. And make a commitment, beginning today, to live differently. Let the Holy Spirit energize you to respect your husband because you love God.

Fourth, to respect our husbands is to make decisions together with them. We show respect to our husbands when we turn to them in making decisions. If we truly respect our husbands, we will consult them before we make decisions that will affect our marriage. Godly wives seek the advice of their husbands, who are their heads, for deliberation about things that they plan to do. An authoritative wife will not consider her husband's ideas when she chooses to make a decision. This goes all the way back to the curse in Genesis: "The Lord said to the woman, 'Your desire shall be for your husband and he shall rule over you'" (Genesis 3:16c NKJV).

A godly wife must have a loving and submissive attachment to her husband that nothing can break. When we become wives, we no longer depend on our parents or friends to make decisions for our marriage; we depend on our husbands. Marriage is designed to be a sphere of mutual dependence between our husbands and us. Think again about the body analogy: can you imagine a body making decisions independently of its head?

When we respect our husbands, they will be admired before the family, church, and society. Think about the impact of this for a moment! What would happen if we diligently practiced these divine instructions, beginning today? The answer is clear and simple. There would not be any marriage quarrels, separations, or divorces. Our families would be like a foretaste of heaven.

Fifth, to respect our husbands is to praise them. Most of the time, human beings do not respond well to criticism. Some wives know how to criticize their husbands for what they do not do well in marriage, but they do not praise their husbands for the things they *do* well. A husband will always respond well to the praises of his wife. God can help us focus on the positive so that we may praise our husbands.

"If you want to motivate your husband's growth as a loving leader, focus on the things he is doing well and praise him. And please don't wait for perfection before you offer praise. Commend him for his effort even if his performance is not up to your expectation. The fastest way to influence quality performance is to express appreciation for past performance."[12]

Living in a way that is respectful to our husbands does not diminish our personality as wives. Instead, such an attitude demonstrates that we value our husbands the same way God values them. Do not be among the foolish wives who do not recognize the importance of their husbands and therefore forfeit their opportunity to experience a good marriage. Respect your husband in private, respect him before your children, and respect him in public. Doing so is good medicine for our marriages! Husbands whose wives show respect to them feel good about themselves and will be motivated to try harder to love their wives.

Our challenge is to look for biblical ways to respect our husbands. Then we get to wait and see how they will be willing to die for us.

Respect Is Mutual

Ultimately, respect must be mutual in marriage. Mutual respect in marriage means both the husband and the wife respect one another. God's image in the husband and wife demand that they live with each other respectfully—and indeed, that is the teaching of the whole Bible for all relationships. "Do to others whatever you would like them to do to you. This is the essence of all that is taught in the law and the prophets" (Matthew 7:12).

We become wives when we respect our husbands.

MAKING A HOME
FOR OUR HUSBANDS

*". . . to live wisely and be pure, to work in their homes,
to do good, and to be submissive to their husbands. Then they
will not bring shame on the word of God."*
—TITUS 2:5

*"It's better to live alone in the corner of an attic
than with a quarrelsome wife in a lovely home."*
—PROVERBS 21:9

*"A wise woman builds her home but a foolish woman
tears it down with her own hands."*
—PROVERBS 14:1

Prior to coming into my marriage, I made a commitment to God and to myself to make my home a place where my husband would want to live. I consider my home to be a place where we can find refuge from the turmoil of the world. God molds me daily with a loving and peaceful spirit to live wisely with my husband. I agree with God to do good and be submissive to my loving husband with the help of His Spirit.

One day, Frantz said this to me: "Djenny, you are truly a blessing from God to me. I want you to know that I always look forward to coming home from work because you make it a comforting and peaceful place for me to dwell. I am thankful to God for giving you to me."

I value my husband's appreciation for what God is doing in my life to live for his glory. Nevertheless, my heartfelt desire is to hear these words from my Savior Jesus when our earthly journey ends: "Well done, my good and faithful servant. You have been faithful in handling this small amount, so now I will give you many more responsibilities. Let's celebrate together!" (Matthew 25:23 NKJV).

I do not pretend that I am a perfect wife to my husband, but I want to be all that God expects of me in my marriage. As a woman, I want to encourage you to work with God to live wisely and purely with your husband even when he does not deserve that. God will honor your efforts and reward you at the end for living for him.

We opened this chapter with a passage from the epistle to Titus. Let's look at it now and explore some of the behavioral skills we can use to make a home for our husbands. It says that women are "to live wisely and be pure, to work in their homes, to do good, and to be submissive to their husbands. Then they will not bring shame on the word of God" (Titus 2:5).

The context of the passage does not suggest that wives cannot work outside their homes. The women to whom these words were addressed were busybodies, and thus they did not prioritize their homes. We read in 1 Timothy 5:13 about the behavior of some of the younger widows: "And if they are on the list [of widows financially supported by the church], they will learn to be lazy and will spend their time gossiping from house to house, meddling in other people's business and talking about things they shouldn't."

The husband provides the means to buy or build a house for the family. However, the wife is the *maker* of the home. A home is not a home without the wife! She makes the house a home for her husband to stay—a home he desires to dwell in; a home he looks forward to being in. The wife is the manager of the home, so the home will be what she wants it to be. In essence, the wife is the keeper of the home and the one who takes care of its affairs. This isn't just a cultural thing; it's built into human nature!

Ladies, the heavenly blessings of fulfilling our responsibilities at home are worth more than the monetary gain and personal fulfillment we may gain if we discharge ourselves from them. The Word of God will be shamed and blasphemed when a wife chooses the world over her own household (Titus 2: 5b). A wife might need to work outside the home to help support the family, but that should not be done to the detriment of her marital responsibilities.

After being a wife and mother, the third role of the woman in the family is described explicitly in the Bible: "To be discreet, chaste, homemakers, good, obedient to their husbands that the word of God may not be blasphemed" (Titus 2:5 NKJV).

How does the wife become a homemaker—literally a *homemaker*, one who makes a home—for her husband? She does this by being discreet (self-controlled), chaste (causing reverence, pure from carnality), good (joyful, agreeable, pleasant, excellent, upright), and submissive to her own husband. Such a godly attitude will keep the husband at home. Some husbands prefer to spend time in other places because of the unfriendly attitude of their wives. Their homes are no longer a pleasant place to stay. We need to make our home a desirable and pleasant place for our husband through our conduct, our words, and our character.

There is no greater responsibility and privilege in the world than to build a home! A home is not a home if its mistress is going from place to place meddling in other people's business.

The effect of sin causes misery in so many families. Many wives reverse God's principles for the family, choosing instead to live by the principles of the world. A Christian wife should have a worldview and conduct that is essentially different from the non-Christian wife, especially in the domain of the home. We need to understand that it is a divine service to work in our homes because it brings glory to God. God has given to the man the responsibility to work hard and provide for the needs of his family, whereas as wives, we have the mission to be attached to our husbands and to serve as the primary caregivers of our children. William Barclay wrote, "How many men, who have set their marks upon the world, have been enabled to do so simply because there was someone at home who cared for him, loved him, and tended to him? It is infinitely more significant that a mother be at home to put her children to bed and to hear them say their prayers than that she should attend all the public and church meetings in the world."

Asking wives to work in their homes does not mean that they cannot have a job. But whatever they choose to do outside their homes, it should not be a threat to their marriage. Women who spend most of their time elsewhere may bring shame to the Word of God as revealed in Titus 2:5. The task of rearing a family and making a home is more rewarding and satisfying than anything else the world might have to offer. Of course, there is always the danger that a wife who chooses not to work outside the home can become idle, drifting from house to house at the expense of her own home and family. God's Word addresses this problem as well, as we have already read. The beauty and joy that can be found within a Christian home are priceless. A respectable wife will live in such a way that her marriage and family do not become a disgrace to God and man.

Skills for Building a Home

Several skills are important for us to make homes for our husbands and families. *First, we must be competent organizers.* Some women are naturally good organizers. Others need to learn how to become effective and competent organizers. In the home, all must be done in order. Our home should be one of beauty, harmony, and order.

A disorganized house does not reflect God's beauty. It is displeasing and frustrating to the family and to those who visit the home—not to mention displeasing and frustrating to ourselves! It is hard to find things when we do not organize our house, is it not? Searching for things because of a lack of organization is a waste of precious time. If our house is a messy place with an atmosphere of pandemonium, we can be certain that it will have a negative impact on our relationships. God is not a God of mess and confusion (1 Corinthians 14:33). I know some of us may not have time to focus on the house as a priority, but it is worth trying to make our house a clean and organized place. It is important also to mention that sometimes the home is messy because we are helping our husbands with other things. In that case, we need to discuss the problem with our husbands to find a solution that counts for both of us.

Good organization requires at least three things. First, we need God's presence. We must cultivate God's presence through studying his Word and fellowshipping with his Spirit. God is a God of order, and his presence in our lives will help us bring order to the home around us. Second, we should have a work schedule. A work schedule will allow us to accomplish our household objectives. If there is no plan, our projects will fail, especially if we are also dealing with other demands and needs. Third, we should establish priorities. We cannot accomplish everything we plan to do at the same time. Therefore, it is necessary for us as wives to establish priorities in our homes.

We need to analyze our activities according to two different measures: importance and urgency. The story of creation is the supreme example of getting things done in this order (Genesis 1; 2:1–3, 15). God created the universe in various parts according to order of importance. Even though he is eternal and all-powerful, he limited himself to creating each part of the universe within a twenty-four-hour block of time. God did not try to create everything in one day. He established priority as to what should be created first.

Just as God established a six-day timetable to create the universe, we must also establish schedules to prioritize our lives. He set a pattern for us to follow. It would be difficult—even impossible—for us to achieve everything we need to get done within twenty-four hours. We must decide what is of ultimate importance and do the rest later. We often say that we do not have enough time to pray, to read the Bible, and to serve God. That it is not true! *The truth of the matter is we have no more nor less than twenty-four hours per day.* It is not the time we do not have that should concern us, but rather, that we have not learned to use our seconds, our minutes, and our hours wisely. We need to worship God first, and we must care for his interests before anything else.

Second, we need to keep our households with the right attitude. To be good homemakers, we must work joyfully (Proverbs 31:10). Why should we have such an attitude? The reason is simple: because we work for God's glory in our homes. Because of our love for God and family, we cheerfully do our work as though we are working for God himself. (And we are!) Because God is not unjust, he will not forget our good work (Hebrews 6:10). We do all things around the house without complaining because it is God who works in us both to will and to do his good pleasure (Philippians 2:13–14).

Whatever we may be involved in doing—caring for our homes, organizing our family's schedule, preparing meals, eating together with our family—we can do all for the glory of God (1 Corinthians 10:31, Colossians 3:23–25). A joyful attitude indicates that we are victorious in deftly managing our homes.

Victory in one area has a spillover effect. If the Spirit rules our lives in the home, he will also rule our lives in other areas. If we can get victory as makers of our homes, we can also get victory elsewhere. On the other hand, if we do not have self-control when we are washing the dishes, do we think we will have victory over demons? If the activities of our house can keep us in captivity, can you imagine how much damage Satan will be able to do in our lives? God cannot use us in great things if we are not faithful in little things, including cooking, changing the beds, planning the meals, and so on (Luke 16:10). Faithfulness in small things translates into faithfulness in big things, and that means victory in all things!

We need to remember that the atmosphere of our home is the result of our lifestyle and our prayer life. We should not complain when we receive answers to our prayers. What do I mean by that? Well, we ask God for marriage. When he gives us husbands, we complain about them because they are not yet what they ought to be in the relationship. We ask God for children. When he gives them to us, we use them as excuses for why we do not serve him. We need to enjoy *every* activity we do in our house for God. Do not allow Satan to take your joy away. Do not complain when you are working for God within your home.

Third, we need to be present in our homes. Frequently, we are so caught up in the cares of life, captured by church work, professional careers, and social activities, that the children suffer from a lack of our affection, presence, instruction, and discipline. Our husbands likewise may suffer from the lack of our presence and attention. We need to be there for our families, giving them our time, attention, and emotional support. It is also necessary for us to watch over family devotions. Along with our husbands (who are the priests of the home), we must create a family altar where the family meets every day for the reading of the Scriptures and prayer.

Many parents have had to sadly confess to a son or a daughter who has rebelled simply because Daddy and Mommy were never there for them. This does not always mean their parents are physical absent: when the father and the mother work all day and then run here and there, or spend their evenings just watching TV or being on the computer, the children will suffer. These are major causes of absence even when everyone is actually in the home. When we are not there, it opens the door for our children to disappear in their search for love, acceptance, and a sense of belonging. A woman's absence from her home is very costly to her family. In our society today, many wives are more bureaucratic than domestic, but it should not be this way for Christian wives. The Bible makes it clear that sometimes a wife may have to work in order to help support her family, but that should not be to the detriment of her husband, her children, or her home. Our main activity is within our marriage and our home (Proverbs 31:10–31, Titus 2:3–5).

When father and mother are absent from the home, the children will pay the consequences. We only have one opportunity to raise our children, but we can have many opportunities to work. Once the opportunity to raise our children passes, we will never get it again. Parents who value the souls of their children more than the gains of this world will be a blessing to humanity. As wives and mothers, we must know that our first responsibility is toward God and our second is to our marriage and our family at home. It is generally unwise for a mother to work outside the home, especially when the children will be neglected or left alone to let our ungodly culture raise them.

Fourth, cooking healthy meals is an essential skill for making a home. A wife and mother cares for her family in the way she plans and prepares the family's meals. In a sense, when we prepare the food, we control the health of our husbands and our children as well as their physical development. We must carefully choose ingredients for the meals we cook so that our husbands and children do not get ill. For example, if the meals are too high in fat, the family will have too much cholesterol in their bodies, which will cause blood problems. Liver illness can come from foods that are high in cholesterol. Salty foods can also cause very serious illnesses— and of course, sugar can do the same! We can definitely benefit from serving good foods. This may help to prevent certain long-term diseases and problems such as heart disease, stroke, and diabetes. It may also help us to keep a healthy weight. In general, a balanced amount of vegetables, fruits, starches, and proteins is considered to be a healthy diet.

God created the family in order to preserve that which is truly valuable in life. Our civilization has quickly deteriorated because it grants less and less attention to our marriages and our children. We should be mindful of that old saying: "The hand that rocks the cradle also governs the world." God made the family a favorable place for the spiritual and physical development of its members. In order for someone to be a leader in the church or in society at large, you must be a good leader at home. How you lead in the church will be a reflection of how responsible you are in your own home. The Bible describes a church leader as "one who rules his own house well, having his children in submission with all reverence (for if a man does not know how to rule his own house, how will he take care of the church of God?)" (1 Timothy 3:4–5). When we do not work together with our husbands to manage our homes well, we will disqualify ourselves from playing a role in the managerial activities of the kingdom of God.

As women, we must keep in mind that God has first called us to become wives to our husbands and second to become mothers to our children. To become a wife to your husband, as we have seen, is to support, respect, and honor him, to provide a comfortable home for him, and to satisfy his sexual needs. It is to do for our husbands what no other woman can or should do for them.

We become wives when we make a home to be present with our husbands.

BEING THE STRENGTH
OF OUR HUSBANDS

"Who can find a virtuous and capable wife?
She is more precious than rubies. Her husband can trust her,
and she will greatly enrich his life. She brings him good,
not harm all the days of her life."
—PROVERBS 31:10–12

The most important question about a good wife is asked in Proverbs 31:10: "Who can find a virtuous wife? For her worth is far above rubies." *Virtuous* refers to all forms of excellence. As virtuous wives, we represent all forms of excellence to our husbands. This entails moral integrity, goodness, and purity. As such, we become the moral and spiritual strength or power to help our husbands carry out the demands of our marriage and other responsibilities of life. God gave us to our husbands to empower them morally and spiritually, enabling them to have courage to withstand the attacks of Satan on our marriages and our lives.

Since virtuous wives are gifts from God, our strength comes from our relationship with God. We read in Isaiah 41:10 these wonderful promises of God: "Don't be afraid, for I am with you. Don't be discouraged, for I am your God. I will strengthen you and help you. I will hold you up with my victorious right hand."

Strength and Virtue

How do we strengthen our husbands? *First, we make them rich—we are more valuable to our husbands than any earthly treasures they may*

144

possess. We read in Proverbs 31:10b that virtuous wives are more valuable to their husbands than rubies. Rubies are precious stones, which in biblical times were a force in the sense of monetary value, durability, and beauty. We are told that *our* worth is far above rubies. Our presence in the lives of our husbands makes them strong, handsome, precious, powerful, and durable. It does not matter how valuable precious stones are, or how beautiful and durable they can be, *we mean more to our husbands.* Rubies are far less valuable than the blessings we give our men.

Godly wives are the strength and resiliency of their husbands. Satan knows that, and so one of his schemes is to use wives like he used Eve in Paradise to destroy the husband and damage God's plan for marriage. Don't be one of those wives! Don't let Satan utilize your strength to destroy your own husband. You should instead let God's Spirit use you to empower your husband to enhance the cause of God's kingdom. Behind a good husband, you will find a Spirit-led wife whose strength is indispensable for the success of the marriage.

God also equips us with his wisdom to help guide our husbands in making decisions for our family. As women, we are gifted with God-given abilities to know certain truths without the assistance of reason like our husbands usually need. God made us this way. Our brains make connections that a man's brain often will not. Our minds work nonstop, building connections in many different ways, so we unconsciously know things without reasoning. For example, when a wife tells her husband, "I don't think what you plan to do will work," many times she is right even though she may not be able to explain why. For her it is about how she feels, not how she thinks about it. Her gut feeling—her intuition—tells her what will or will not work. Many husbands would have spared their lives from much misery if they had listened to their wives! God designed these differences so husband and wife can complement each other.

When we accept the teachings of God, we become the length of days for our husbands (Proverbs 3:1–3). This is basically saying we should not

kill our husbands with our character and conduct! Instead, our positive
influence in our husbands' lives will contribute to their longevity as God
ordained. We know that the Bible says wicked people die before their
time (Psalm 55:23, Ecclesiastes 7:17). To lengthen the days of our husbands is to become their moral strength in order that they may live the
number of days God has ordained for them.

We are the riches and honor of our husbands. Our methods of dealing with our husbands should be methods of pleasantness, happiness,
and peace. We should be a tree of life to them. By our wisdom, we can
shape and establish our husbands. As virtuous wives, we need to open
our mouths with wisdom and let kindness be the law of our tongues so
that we may strengthen our husbands (Proverbs 31:26).

*Second, we are trustworthy—we become the strength of our husbands
because we are wives whom they can trust.* We read in Proverbs 31:11–12
these amazing words: "The heart of her husband safely trusts her; so he
will have no lack of gain. She does him good and not evil all the days of
her life"(NKJV). God in us makes us trustworthy wives. Our husbands
trust in us, making our relationship with them safe. Being consistently
good and faithful to our husbands in what we say and do for them will
surely give them grounds to trust us. But if we make up our mind to do
evil to our husbands, we cannot expect their trust.

A trustworthy person is someone you can rely on. Can your husband
lean on you heavily without fear of falling down? Like a baby who trusts
his mother for everything, our husbands should trust us in everything
because we are virtuous wives. Our character and conduct should not
give our husbands any reason not to trust us. If we have not been trustworthy, we must seek God's help and the forgiveness of our husbands.
If the romance in our marriage has stopped because of past failures that
made us hard to trust, we can begin today to restore that trust. It may
take time, but we can do the good things that characterized our relationship in the early stages of falling in love. Rising up early while it is yet
night to provide food for our husbands and watching over our ways in

the household will build trust. Trust grows as we do good to our husbands. Our husbands will praise us, and our children will call us blessed.

The greatest good we can do to our husbands is to live in the fear of the Lord in our relationship with them. Charm is deceitful and beauty is passing, but if we fear God we shall be praised and live long (Proverbs 31:15, 27–28, 30).

Third, we become the strength of our husbands when we give them a good reputation. Building our husband's reputation takes time and effort. The long process of giving either a good or a bad reputation to our husbands begins with what we say about them to others and with how we live with our husbands. We must cherish and value our reputation as virtuous wives and the good reputation we build for our husbands. We can recover from much earthly loss fairly easily, but the loss of reputation is hard to recover. Yet with God's grace we can build a new reputation with a changed life and give hope to many. Helping our husbands have a good reputation can attract others to God.

As virtuous wives, our character and conduct should speak well of our husbands in the community in which we live, among our coworkers and friends, in the local church where we are ministering, in the country, around the world, and most importantly, in heaven where our heavenly Father dwells. We should live in such a way that people think highly of our husbands. For example, speaking well of our husbands in public, helping them to dress in a way that's clean and organized, assisting them with language proficiency so they can be good public speakers, and encouraging them to study and obey God's Word can create a wealth of good reputation for them.

The reputation of our husbands is one of the good qualifications they need to become leaders, to get and keep a job, and to live an honorable life. Every good thing we do in life requires a good reputation. "A good name is to be chosen rather than great riches" (Proverbs 22:1 NKJV). We are to be concerned about both God's reputation and our husband's reputation in the ways we live with them at home, at church, and everywhere we might go.

The Strength of the Spirit

A virtuous woman is the moral force of her husband. We become wives to our husbands not to use our moral strength to trash them, but to lift them up with humility and kindness. We do that not because we feel like it, nor for our own pleasure, but because it is the right thing to do in the Lord. We are the helpers God has provided to assist our husbands to be all that they should be in Christ Jesus. Our becoming the moral force of our husbands is the ground for our dream marriage to become real. Let's go, wives! We have all the resources available in Jesus that we need to be the virtuous wives God has designed us to be. We dare not allow immoral cultural influences to corrupt our virtues in Christ Jesus. Let's keep our eyes on God, stay planted in his Word, and live as the strength of our husbands.

The answer to the question "Who can find a virtuous wife?" is that a virtuous wife is a gift from God. *You are a gift from God to your husband.* Earthly treasures cannot buy such a wife, because she is more valuable than any earthly treasure. She is from above. If any woman wants to be a virtuous wife, she needs to be a heart in which God's Spirit can dwell and a life he can control.

If you have not been surrendered to the Spirit of God in the past, you can begin to be a virtuous wife today. With the indwelling presence of the Spirit of God, you can be what you must be. You can be assured of that blessed presence by hearing, believing, and trusting the truth which is Jesus Christ (John 14:6). He is the embodiment of the truth. When you believe and trust in Jesus, God will seal you with his Spirit (Romans 5:5, Ephesians 1:13–14). Jesus has asked God the Father to give the Holy Spirit to anyone who trusts him for eternal life (John 14:15–18), and God gives that gift gladly! God's Spirit is proof that we belong to Christ Jesus (Romans 8:9).

Everything God asks us to do is done in the context of a Spirit-filled life. We become wives when we become the moral strength of our husbands, and our relationship with God makes that possible.

INFLUENCING OUR HUSBANDS FOR GOD

"In the same way, you wives must accept the authority of your husbands. Then, even if some refuse to obey the Good News, your godly lives will speak to them without any words. They will be won over by observing your pure and reverent lives."
—1 PETER 3:1–2

To the same degree that I let God influence my life, I influence my husband. I cannot give my husband anything good unless I receive it from my relationship with God. Thus, it is vital for me to maintain my fellowship with the Lord daily as I study and obey his Word with the help of his Spirit who lives in me.

As godly wives, we have the privilege of influencing our husbands for God. We do this in the context of our relationship with them. When I notice that my husband prioritizes others over our relationship, I do a loving deed to help him see that. I make him his favorite meal and invite him to go on a romantic date to rekindle our love for one another. This has been working very well for us. To encourage my loving efforts, Frantz said to me, "Your love for God, for me, and for our daughters has greatly influenced me to love you more and more. You are consistently exemplifying God's love for me in the way you talk with me and conduct yourself. You serve and appreciate me daily even when I do not deserve it. And when you fall short of living for God's glory, you acknowledge it and ask for forgiveness. I see God's love in you, my darling."

His encouraging words inspire me to grow more in love and knowledge of God. With God's help, you and I can use the power of influence to surprise and encourage our husbands with our godly conduct.

As wives, we are essential to the success of our marriages. We can influence positive change in our husbands for God's glory. In order for us to be effective influencers and help our husbands change in positive ways, we must focus on nurturing the incorruptible spiritual beauty we received at conversion from God through faith in Christ Jesus. In this way, we can influence our husbands whether they are living for God or not. Those who love God will be influenced to serve him more effectively. Those who do not love God can be moved by our conduct to seek him out and become changed men.

A Gentle and Quiet Spirit

First Peter 3:3-4 tells women, "Don't be concerned about the outward beauty of fancy hairstyles, expensive jewelry, or beautiful clothes. You should clothe yourselves instead with the beauty that comes from within, the unfading beauty of a gentle and quiet spirit, which is so precious to God."

This does not mean that all women should have a quiet or mousy personality! *A gentle and quiet spirit is a moral ability the Holy Spirit gives us to trust God to control the events and situations in our lives, knowing that he will work all things out to transform us into the likeness of our Lord Jesus Christ (Romans 8:28-30).* A quiet spirit implies a loving character. It does not suppress our true personality or take the fun parts of life. I find my value and true identity in knowing what God does for me in Christ Jesus. I like what Matthew Henry says about what it means to be a gentle or meek woman. He said, "Meekness is the silent submission of the soul to the 'providence' of God concerning us."

With a quiet and gentle spirit, we can influence our husbands to desire our God. A quiet and gentle spirit is one of the byproducts of the work of the Spirit of God in our lives (Galatians 5:22). If we allow ourselves to be led by the devil, you can bet we will be lousy wives! But if the Spirit of God leads us, we will be gentle and gracious. A quiet and gentle spirit will create a godly personality in us, which helps us to be confident helpers rather than insecure manipulators. We trust in God by acknowledging him in what we do and say to our husbands. Trusting fully in God, we believe that God alone can make our husband what he should be in the marriage. We deliberately, carefully, and humbly choose our words to communicate the truth in love to our husbands. We live in faith rather than fear because we know God is in perfect control of our lives.

A quiet and gentle spirit is the most important beauty we can possess. With this spiritual beauty, we can be the lenses through which our husbands see God. Many marriage relationships become confrontational and quarrelsome rather than peaceful. It is a blessing to have a peaceful marriage (Matthew 5:9, Romans 12:18). It is well documented in the Bible that a quarrelsome person can lead to separation. We read in Proverbs 21:9 these alarming words: "It's better to live alone in the corner of an attic than with a quarrelsome wife in a lovely home." Proverbs 12:18 says, "Some people make cutting remarks, but the words of the wise bring healing."

In our words and actions, we can cultivate peace in our homes. God wants to help wives to "live wisely and be pure, to work in their homes, to do good, and to be submissive to their husbands. Then they will not bring shame on the word of God" (Titus 2:5). It is God's will for wives to "be respected and not slander others. They must exercise self-control and be faithful in everything they do" (1 Timothy 3:11). In other words, we should be women of peace who bring peace in our homes and marriages.

Good Conduct

Through the help of God controlling our minds, emotions, and actions, we can absolutely be a good influence to our husbands. God has prepared good works in Christ Jesus for us to practice (Ephesians 2:10). With the anointing of God upon him, Jesus went everywhere and did good to people (Acts 10:38). Because of Jesus's goodness, many people who were oppressed by the power of the devil were healed. Our good conduct, under the anointed power of the Spirit, can likewise save our husbands from demonic and worldly influences.

As we receive, meditate on, and practice the goodness of God in our lives, it will overflow in the ways we are good to our husbands. If we truly believe God is good all the time, then his goodness should makes us good wives as well. Being good to our husbands can lead them to wonder about our God.

As we do the "good works" laid out for us, we can serve our husbands with a Christlike attitude. We can do good to our husbands when they do not deserve it to display God's grace to them. We can pray for our husbands and pray with our husbands. We can make allowance to forgive our husbands when they sin against us, just as God forgave us, and we can be kind to our husbands with the kindness of God. We can listen to our husbands respectfully, understanding and satisfying their emotional and spiritual needs. Jesus is the example of what good conduct is all about. Looking at the life of Jesus in the Bible, we can learn how to be good to our husbands.

We have a serious responsibility to be good to our husbands. Be careful! Remember that our strength can be turned against our husbands if we listen to the devil instead of God. Satan influenced Eve to bring down her husband and cast him out of Paradise. He used Delilah to deceive Samson into giving up his power. He used Solomon's many wives to influence him to worship their false gods. (See Genesis 3, Judges 16, and 1 Kings 11.) If we are not careful, Satan will use us also to destroy our husbands and our marriages. The devil is seeking whom he may devour (1 Peter 5:8). We need to be on our guard not to let him use us to keep our husbands away from a relationship with God. Instead, we need to let the Spirit of God use us to do good to our husbands and to draw them closer to God. God saved us to be good our husbands.

Living with the Devil

Our wish for you is that you live with a husband who loves God and who models the love of Christ to you in your marriage. However, we realize that for some wives, the story is very different. If you are trying to influence your husband for God, but he is not open or willing to obey God, we want to give you a few words of encouragement here.

Saul was the first king of the Jewish nation. Although God had called and blessed him, he disobeyed God to please himself and the people (1 Samuel 13:5-14; 15:1-35). Instead of acknowledging and confessing his sin, he attempted to justify his evildoing. God gave Saul time to repent, but he refused. Because of Saul's continuous rebellious attitude, God rejected him and anointed David to become king of the Israelites.

Because Saul rejected God's leadership and grace toward him and his family, he opened his life up to be influenced by the devil. He no longer had the protection of God from Satan and his evil spirits. God allowed an evil spirit to come into the life of Saul to torment him. Since an evil spirit possessed Saul, his heart became a place of hatred and jealousy. He plotted to murder David, although David loved and respected him as the anointed king.

God put his Spirit in David and gave him musical skill to help Saul. When David did not play music with the anointing of God for Saul, the king's situation was awful. David was the solution to Saul's problem. However, Saul wanted to eliminate David. In spite of Saul's evil attitude toward him, David dealt with him in love. Whenever he could, he played music to calm the king down when the evil spirit tormented him. Even when David was forced to run from Saul, he continued to bless and protect the king (see 1 Samuel 16; 1 Samuel 24).

Perhaps your husband has been influenced by evil spirits to live with you like the devil. Perhaps your spouse wants to get rid of you though you are his gift from God, like Saul who wanted to kill David though David was the solution to his problem. Perhaps your husband does not yet see your value as a godly wife. Don't be discouraged, and don't try to get even with him. Do not give access to the devil. Instead, let the Holy Spirit use you to calm your husband down, like God used David to calm the rejected king.

Like David did, there is a time when a wife must leave a bad relationship to protect herself from a physically abusive husband. She can continue to love, serve, and honor her husband while running away to preserve her own life. This is a loving act to compel a husband to seek marital counseling and learn the behavioral and cognition skills he needs to cope more effectively with the problems that all good relationships face. God did not create marriage to be violent, but respectful and loving. Respecting your husband does not mean letting him get away with persistent maladaptive behaviors. Tolerating cruelty in marriage negatively reinforces destructive conduct.

In most cases, however, a marriage's problems will not necessitate leaving. No matter what our situation, we need to lean not on our wisdom to solve our problems, but on God to work it out for his glory. Making it our priority to trust God wholeheartedly is vital. We can be like our Lord Jesus, who knew Judas Iscariot was going to betray him but loved him just as he loved the other disciples who remained loyal to him. Jesus wanted to please his Father. He trusted God the Father with the consequences of his obedience. Obey your heavenly Father, and trust him with the rest.

"Trust in the Lord with all your heart; do not depend on your own understanding. Seek his will in all you do, and he will show you which path to take. Don't be impressed with your own wisdom. Instead, fear the Lord and turn away from evil. Then you will have healing for your body and strength for your bones. Honor the Lord with your wealth and with the best part of everything you produce. Then he will fill your barns with grain, and your vats will overflow with good wine. My child, don't reject the Lord's discipline, and don't be upset when he corrects you. For the Lord corrects those he loves, just as a father corrects a child in whom he delights" (Proverbs 3:5–12).

If your husband is not living according to the Holy Spirit, you will experience the negative effects. You already know that, no doubt! Your husband is connected with you in marriage, and you live in the same house with him. God understands your situation, and he alone can help you. Like God helped and protected David who trusted him, he will protect you. Don't be troubled when your husband is troubled. Instead, trust God and seek counseling from godly counselors to help you cope with your personal and marital problems.

God wants to use you to influence your husband so that he can live for his glory. Greater is the Spirit of God who is in you than the evil spirits that are in the world (1 John 4:4). Don't be intimidated by evil, but overcome evil by doing good with the help of the Holy Spirit.

A FINAL WORD FOR WIVES

It seems that most women go into marriage thinking it will be easy to help their husbands. After all, they're in love, right? But after the wedding ceremony is over, those wives face the reality of what their husbands are really are all about. They thought their husbands were going to continue to be the loving men they were during the courtship. But when reality settles into the home, many husbands become bossy, arrogant, dominant, and uncooperative. They drive their wives just like they drive their cars.

At that point, some wives still try to help, but with no success. Others just quit on their husbands because they cannot handle the mess. Still others remain in the marriage, but against their will. They live unhappily because the struggle for control is evident in their marriage. Unfortunately, ungodly husbands have used religion to turn marriage into their own kingdom where they can rule over their wives. *That is not what God wants for marriage. That is not his design, and it is not true religion.* He wants and gives good relationships to mankind. God created men and women to dominate the earth together, not men to dominate their wives. God alone is entitled to rule over mankind, because he is just and good.

God made the husband and the wife to walk side by side in obedience to him. He made the wife to be a suitable helper to her husband. However, it's a fact that some husbands do not view their wives as helping partners in marriage. They look at their wives as followers instead of their companions. Those husbands think they can do whatever they want, and their wives must obey them. That is not biblical at all. No man should enter into marriage with such a false worldview if he wants to have a successful marriage. God has established the rules of marriage by which husbands and wives must live. They are not in marriage to please their selfish desires, but to glorify God, who is the giver of marriage. If the harshness and sinful conduct of a husband have any benefit, they are only for Satan. They have no benefits for marriage, humanity, or God's kingdom.

What a wife needs to understand about helping her husband, then, is that it can be hard to be the type of helper God wants her to be if the husband refuses to obey the lordship of Jesus Christ. Rebellious husbands are difficult to help! A wife needs to understand that reality and deal with it according to God's Word.

What should a wife do with a rebellious husband? The natural reaction is to dump him, but that is not what our primary response should be. *Instead, the wife should focus on what God wants her to do.* A husband who presented himself as a lamb before marriage can turn himself into a lion in marriage. At that point, the wife should no longer rely on the love of her husband to live her life. She should rather rely on God's Word. If a worldly husband hates his wife, she must remember the world hated Jesus also (John 15:18). Suffering is a part of what God has called us to. Jesus suffered, and he is our example. We have to follow in his footsteps. "He never sinned, nor ever deceived anyone. He did not retaliate when He was insulted, nor threaten revenge when He suffered. He left His case in the hands of God, who always judges fairly" (1 Peter 2:22–23). Jesus came to help us, just as wives come to help their husbands. His help to us came with unfair treatment. He suffered for doing what was right, and he never complained. Jesus always turned to God who judges fairly.

As a wife tries to help her husband, she should keep in mind that helping him might come with unfair treatment, just as it happened to Jesus. For the sake of pleasing God like Jesus did, the wife must turn to her Shepherd, the Guardian of her soul, for comfort and direction. It is not humanly possible for a wife to live with a husband who is stubborn and rebellious. She needs the help of God.

The road of obedience to God may involve suffering for Him. "For God called you to do good, even if it means suffering, just as Christ suffered for you. He is your example, and you must follow in his steps" (1 Peter 2:21). We are not suggesting by any means that a wife should allow her husband to cause her harm. It is always good to seek help when we cannot solve our own problems before a situation worsens. Sadly, some women stay in ungodly and abusive relationships, hoping their husbands will eventually change without learning problem-solving skills. This is not wise. These relationships can end in destructive consequences for the whole family, including homicide.

As godly wives, when our husbands don't obey God, we must not join them. We should rather go on living for God. "In the same way, you wives must accept the authority of your husbands. Then, even if some refuse to obey the Good News, your godly lives will speak to them without any words. They will be won over by observing your pure and reverent lives. Don't be concerned about the outward beauty of fancy hairstyles, expensive jewelry, or beautiful clothes. You should clothe yourselves instead with the beauty that comes from within, the unfading beauty of a gentle and quiet spirit, which is so precious to God. This is how the holy women of old made themselves beautiful. They trusted God and accepted the authority of their husbands. For instance, Sarah obeyed her husband, Abraham, and called him her master. You are her daughters when you do what is right without fear of what your husbands might do" (1 Peter 3:1–6).

No wife can live the biblical requirements for a marriage without being filled with the Holy Spirit. God knows it is hard for a wife to live with an ungodly husband. Therefore, he gives the wife his Spirit, who is the great Helper, to help her out. A wife is not alone in the battle as she sometimes seems to be. A wife who is a child of God has the Spirit of God living in her to comfort, help, and lead her into all truth.[13]

Let God be your helper so that you may help your husband. Pray with the psalmist: "Come with great power, O God, and rescue me! Defend me with Your might. Listen to my prayer, O God. Pay attention to my plea. For strangers are attacking me; violent people are trying to kill me. They care nothing for God. But God is my helper. The Lord keeps me alive! May the evil plans of my enemies be turned against them. Do as You promised and put an end to them" (Psalms 54:1–5).

Do not worry, but pray to your heavenly Father (Philippians 4:6–9). God helped Hannah when she was in deep anguish (1 Samuel 1:1–18). He can help you too—and don't forget to praise him as Hannah did (1 Samuel 2:1–11)!

Although individual marriages can be difficult, there is always hope. God's design for marriage is good—very good. I love my marriage. God blesses it with his abiding presence through faith in Christ Jesus. I thank God for giving me a wonderful husband who loves me just as I am. He strengthens me when I am weak, inspires me when I am down, cooks and serves me with when I am hungry, and laughs with me when I take life too seriously. God knew from eternity that I would need someone like my husband to be in my life so that I may become what our heavenly Father wants me to be. Every day I pray that God will keep the amazing and strong marital relationship we enjoy together going until we meet him in glory. The feeling of being loved by my husband can compare to none other. We draw the good qualities we need to complete each other from our relationships with God, our Creator and Designer of marriage.

I know for sure that I am not the exception. The good news is that many couples are experiencing and living good marriages because they value their moral commitment to each other and to God. The spend quality time together, being friends to one another, respecting the individuality of each other, and counting each others' needs. They work together to solve their problems. They share ethical values; they have faith, hope, and love; and they see themselves as one with God in accomplishing his purposes for marriage.

If you have not yet lived your dream marriage, don't lose hope. God can empower you and your husband with the good qualities necessary to make it happen. Pray to God to bless your marriage with his presence so that you and your husband can have a triangular relationship with him, one that will truly build a strong marriage.

AFTERWORD

Considering the decline of marriage in our society, it is evident that successful marriages will be possible only when men and women learn how to become husbands and wives to one another as God has prescribed in the Scriptures. Marriage is a triangular covenant relationship between God, the husband, and the wife. In a Christian marriage, both partners agree to enter into a marital relationship and commit themselves to living according to biblical principles that God has established for marriage. That commitment involves self-sacrifice and the enabling power of God's Spirit in order to become a reality. Since God is the maker of marriage, he alone can help husbands and wives experience the marriage he foresaw before the foundation of the world.

When we consider marriage solely as a contract between a man and a woman, we exclude God from the relationship, because a contract by definition is an exchange of goods or a business transaction between two parties. People who adopt the idea that marriage is a contract base their relationships on a materialistic worldview. Since material things expire, they will see their marriages as lasting only as long as the goods are usable. Christians who view their marriages as involving the eternal God will understand that their relationships are meant to last and that God has already provided in Christ Jesus to make that happen!

From the beginning of the marriage story in Genesis 2:4–28, we see provisions God made for husbands and wives. These are called *general provisions* because they are for all people, whether they are Christians or not. These include God's goodness, love, compassion, and mercy. This is what God gave all humanity before the fall of man. God provided everything necessary for the first couple, Adam and Eve, to have a successful marriage. He created a good, safe, and fruitful environment, and he built a home for them. This glorious scene turned into chaos when the first couple invited the devil into their relationship, but God restored them with his love.

In Genesis 1:12–25, we see a repeated theme about the environment God made for men and women: "And God saw that it was good." God made everything good. The environment was also safe because God protected it with his mighty angels. God still protects his people today with his angels (Psalm 34:7; Acts 5:18-19; Hebrews 1:14). Jesus Christ asked God to protect those he has given him (John 17:11-19). Paul's request for prayer of protection, "Pray, too, that we will be rescued from wicked and evil people, for not everyone is a believer (2 Thessalonians 3:2). God's goodness is still available to us. God's goodness and love is for everyone. The Psalmist says, "The Lord is good to everyone. He showers compassion on all his creation" (Psalm 145:9). "In that way, you will be acting as true children of your Father in heaven. For he gives his sunlight to both the evil and the good, and he sends rain on the just and the unjust alike" (Matthew 5:45). Some people choose not to serve God, but he serves them daily because he is good to humanity.

God also gave particular or special provisions for Christians only. These provisions enable us to *practice* the general provisions, including God's goodness and love toward humanity. Some of these special provisions are God's Spirit and his Word, the fellowship of God's people, and fervent prayers. These provisions are designed to help us glorify God in our marriages. To receive the special provisions available to men and women, we must turn to Jesus Christ as our Savior and Lord. Sins prevent us from being what God wants. We must be free from the power and practice of sin in order to live right for God and to make our marriages a place where God's will is done.

In God's design, *goodness* is the basis of every marriage relationship. The husband must speak good words to his wife (Ephesians 4:29), do good acts to his wife (Galatians 6:10), and treat her with goodness and kindness in private and public (Ephesians 4:32, Colossians 3:12). The wife must also do good to her husband, speaking gracious words to him, supporting him, and giving him respect, honor, and kindness. God wants us to be good to our spouses, and this is only possible when God's presence is in our lives. No one is good but God (Mark 10:18). He is the standard of good. He made everything good. God made the man and woman good because he made them in his image (Genesis 1:27). We lost God's goodness in Adam, but God restored his goodness in us through faith in Christ Jesus. Thus, a Christian husband proves he is born into the family of God through the work of the Holy Spirit when he is good to his wife. A wife displays her position as a child of God when she is good to her husband. God's presence in our lives will reveal his goodness in our marriages. To create a good environment for the wife, the husband must accept that God made everything good and that he entrusted his goodness to him to keep and cultivate (Genesis 2:15). As the husband's God-given companion and helper, the wife needs to help her husband preserve the goodness of God in their marriage.

In Christ Jesus, we have everything we need to live in a good, safe, intimate, and deeply loving marriage to reveal God's glory. May we allow the Holy Spirit to help us be men and women who are good husbands and wives!

"Unless the Lord builds a house, the work of the builders is wasted. Unless the Lord protects a city, guarding it with sentries will do no good. It is useless for you to work so hard from early morning until late at night, anxiously working for food to eat; for God gives rest to his loved ones. Children are a gift from the Lord; they are a reward from him. Children born to a young man are like arrows in a warrior's hands. How joyful is the man whose quiver is full of them! He will not be put to shame when he confronts his accusers at the city gates" (Psalm 127).

God builds our marriages on the foundation of Jesus Christ. This requires our obedience and attention. "So why do you keep calling me 'Lord, Lord!' when you don't do what I say? I will show you what it's like when someone comes to me, listens to my teaching, and then follows it. It is like a person building a house who digs deep and lays the foundation on solid rock. When the floodwaters rise and break against that house, it stands firm because it is well built. But anyone who hears and doesn't obey is like a person who builds a house without a foundation. When the floods sweep down against that house, it will collapse into a heap of ruins" (Luke 6:46–49).

God made us male and female to become good husbands and wives in Christ Jesus. For his glory, let's pursue the best marriages we can make. Together, let's discover the goodness of God in marriage and display it to the world.

ENDNOTES

1 Floyd McClung, Jr., *God's Man in the Family* (Eugene, OR: Harvest House Publishers, 1994), 29.

2 Gary J. Oliver, Ph.D., *Real Men Have Feelings Too* (Chicago: Moody Press, 1993), 43.

3 Frantz Lamour, *A Dream Marriage* (Maitland, FL: Xulon Press, 2009), 108–109.

4 Gary J. Oliver, Ph. D., *Real Men Have Feelings Too* (Chicago: Moody Press, 1993), 60.

5 Jerry Cook and Stanley C. Baldwin, *Love, Acceptance & Forgiveness* (Ventura, CA: Regal Books, 1979), 13.

6 Joseph M. Stowell, *Following Christ* (Grand Rapids, MI: Zondervan Publishing House, 1996), 17.

7 James Dobson Dr., *What Wives Wish Their Husbands Knew about Women* (Carol Stream, IL: Tyndale House Publishers, 1975), 13.

8 Stormie Omartian, *The Power of a Praying Husband* (Eugene, OR: Harvest House Publishers, 2001), 114.

9   Scott Haltzman, M.D. and Theresa F. Digeronimo, *The Secrets of Happily Married Men* (San Francisco: Jossey- Bass, 2006), 71.

10 Tim Stafford, *Love, Sex & the Whole Person* (Grand Rapids, MI: Zondervan Publishing House, 1991), 175.

11 Cliff Isaacson and Meg Schneider, *The Good-for-You Marriage* (Avon, MA: Adams Media, 2008), 8.

12 Gary Chapman, Dr., *Five Signs of a Loving Family* (Northfield Publishing; New Edition edition July 13, 1998), 227.

13 Kevin Leman, Dr., *Have a New Husband by Friday* (Rivell a division of Baker Publishing Group, 2009), 39.

14 Rev. Matthew Henry, *A Discourse On Meekness and Quietness of Spirit* (Published by the American Tract Society), 1.

15 Barclay, William. "Commentary on Titus 2:5." ("William Barclay's Daily Study Bible"), http://www.studylight.org/commentaries/dsb/view.cgi?bk=55&ch=2". 1956-1959.

13 [16] Study these Scriptures for help: John 15:26; John 16:5–7; John 12–14; Acts 4:31; Romans 8:1–17, 26–30; Ephesians 1:13–16; Ephesians 3:16; Colossians 1:11; 2 Timothy 1:7; and 1 Peter 5:10.